RANTS, RUMBLES AND ROARS

MOTORCYCLING IN AMERICA

STU SEGAL

COVER PHOTO: Late 1960s. Author and his 1951/58 Harley-Davidson.

This book contains original compositions by the author. Also contained herein are reprints of "The Road" by T.E. Lawrence, and "Song of the Sausage Creature" by Hunter S. Thomson which are in the public domain, as well as some photographs which are in the public domain; those items which are in the public domain are therefore not protected by the copyright of this book.

Print Edition IV/MMXIV/V2

ACKNOWLEDGEMENTS

Stephen H. Segal
Consultant Editor

Paula Grimaldi-Reardon
Photography, pages 91 and 92

To my brothers and sisters in the wind, you know who you are. Back in the day when there were hardly any of us riding I waved to everyone on a bike, you were the one who waved back. When we were caught in a summer hailstorm and ducked under an overpass, you were the one who lent me your towel. When my tire went flat, punctured by a drill bit on the highway, you were the one who rode all over hell's half acre with me on the back until we found an inner tube. And when my transmission disintegrated hundreds of miles from home, you were the one that welded it back together. This book's for you.

This book is also for the crew that was once "Iron Biker News," Bob (Cowboy) Steel, Tom and Lucy McTamney, Loretta Jackson, Gary Introne, and all the other contributors. We never made any money doing Iron Biker, but we sure had a blast going everywhere, meeting people, taking pictures, then writing about it. Best job in the world!

Finally, I dedicate this book to all who discouraged my motorcycling, insisting I was on the wrong path, would never amount to anything, and would likely become a mangled mishap of motorcycle mayhem. Perhaps you should read some Thoreau: "If a man does not keep pace with his companions, perhaps it is because he hears a different drummer. Let him step to the music which he hears, however measured or far away."

Contents

Introduction

When I was perhaps five years old I saw a police officer on a motorcycle and heard the rumble that I now know is a Harley-Davidson—it made an impression. As a young teen, I was in the back seat of my parents' car; we were speeding down the Atlantic City Expressway, a new state-of-the-art superhighway with a 70 mile per hour speed limit, at high speed; suddenly a roar and the flash of chrome as a bearded, long-haired, tattooed man thundered past on a chopper, the distinctive roar slowly diminishing as he faded down the road ahead of us—it made an impression.

Now this was not an impression that made my parents too happy. They were thinking "medical school"; I was thinking Harley, BSA, Triumph.

As soon as I got my driver's license there was one thing on my mind . . . motorcycle. I found a 10-year old big British motorcycle with loud pipes and "apehangers," and so began a lifelong relationship. A relationship which has given me hour upon hour of serenity, taken me places I would have never gone, and introduced me to people I would have never met.

While others were playing softball or going to the movies, I was working on my bike. Twenty years later colleagues were going to the beach or the Caribbean for vacation, I was cruising the highways of America, everything I needed strapped to my sissybar.

When I was nearly 50 the bank where I made my career for a quarter century was sold . . . for the third time . . . and I found myself at a company I couldn't stand. Abandoning a certain future in an industry where I had proven earnings potential, I took a leap of faith into the motorcycle business. 15 years later, my partners and I have owned some of the best motorcycle stores in the U.S., receiving awards and accolades from the public, the industry and the manufacturers.

And along the way, I have written . . . about the bikes, the culture, and the industry. In the late '80s my friend, and later partner, bought a "biker newspaper" from a major publisher and I became a regular contributor, writing both features and columns, for "Iron Biker News."

Then came blogs and social media, where the scope of my writing expanded to politics, culture, entertainment . . . but still occasionally, motorcycles.

What follows are some of my previously published articles, and a few new ones, dealing with the world of motorcycles and motorcycling. The culture, the business, the hobby. I enjoyed writing them, I enjoyed revisiting them, and I enjoyed commenting on them for this book . . . I hope you enjoy them too.

P.S. I am a little embarrassed by some of the things I said years ago and by the writing style. (Much of it is written in the biker voice and style that was so prevalent in '70s and '80s biker publications; thank goodness in all my writing I never once called people my "bros.") My attitudes and outlooks have matured over the years, and my writing has evolved, as you will hopefully see from the new essays in this book. As to the old ramblings, regardless the almost overwhelming urge to edit them, I give them to you as written, unedited, embarrassing though they may be. —Stu

PREFACE

What You Need to Know to Make Heads or Tails of This Book

Let's be clear, when I say "motorcycling" I am talking about riding motorcycles on the street, on public highways. I know there are motorcycles designed to ride off-road, but to me motorcycling has always been about riding on the streets—if I'm off the road, there's a big problem.

To understand this book, one must understand the social context of the world of motorcycling. Recent years would lead one to believe that motorcycling is an accepted activity, accepted alternate form of transportation, and has always been so; this is simply not true. For the majority of the latter half of the 20th century, motorcycling in America was stigmatized by "the establishment."

Two things happened in the late '40s/early '50s that had a profound impact on the way motorcycling, and motorcyclists, were perceived. First, young men returning from World War II, looking for the camaraderie they had become accustomed to in the service; some of them were motorcyclists. Some of these men banded together in informal groups that rode in their spare time, sometimes locally, sometimes traveling. Often times, they "chopped" their motorcycles, taking standard Harley-Davidsons (which were readily available, and looked very much like today's police bikes), removing all excess components, stripping them down to the barest essentials. In fact, these modifications had nothing to do with style (which is what today's choppers are all about), the modifications had to do with making the motorcycle more efficient—faster, better fuel economy, lighter and easier to handle. These men were not ne'er-do-wells, criminals, or troublemakers—they were, however, looking for fun and a good time.

In 1953, Columbia Pictures released "The Wild One," a film depicting a group of these motorcyclists, traveling together and looking for a good time. It starred Marlon Brando in the iconic role of a moody, rebellious, black leather clad biker. It drew on the worst fears of the public, conjuring up a scenario where motorcyclists run amok, and take over a town. So powerful was the story that it created an image of "bikers" that would last for decades. Unfortunately, certain young people actually aspired to that wild image, reinforcing it.

By the mid-50s, the American public largely believed that leather clad motorcyclists were all hoodlums. Additionally, the American Motorcyclist Association unwittingly added to the problem—following an incident in Hollister, California, where some motorcyclists got out of control, the AMA released a statement that "99% of all of their members are law-abiding citizens and only 1% are "outlaw"." Which gave birth to the terms "outlaw biker" and "one percenter," terms which were adopted, embraced, by the worst of the worst criminal motorcyclists.

I started riding in the mid-'60s and, like others, loved the idea of chopped motorcycles. Lighter, faster, better handling. (Not to mention, louder and flashier!) Now I was not, and have never been, a criminal . . . nor have my friends. But by the mid-'60s the public had completely accepted the notion that motorcycle=biker, therefore chopper=criminal biker. Not only the public, also law enforcement.

So when my generation started building bikes and riding we had no idea that we would be so challenged in so many different ways by the public and by law enforcement. Riding a chopper in the '60s could be exciting, and I don't mean in a good way—there was rarely ever a ride that someone didn't try to run us off the road, or that we weren't stopped by the police.

Being stopped by the police never amounted to anything "serious"—and by serious I mean, none of us were ever arrested for outstanding warrants, for carrying weapons, for carrying drugs or for other serious crimes. But we were constantly cited for minor infractions—mufflers too loud, handlebars too high, no inspection sticker, etc. Now, this didn't happen occasionally, it happened daily.

I'm not here to talk about police corruption, but one Atlantic City Police officer would stop me whenever he saw me, and would always find some minor infraction. Then I would take the ticket he issued to another AC officer, a motorcycle officer I knew, and give him $10—magically the ticket got "fixed." (I always wondered if they were in cahoots.) And incidentally, $10 was a lot more 50 years ago when the average price of a new car was $2,650!

This perception that bikers were no good, probably criminals, definitely up to something, went on for decades. But who cared? Who was concerned that "bikers" were being discriminated against? Dirty, greasy, loud bikers, a bane on society.

At some point, and it's not a definite point or event I can identify, this began to change. I believe it was in the late '90s, and was the indirect result of Harley-Davidson cleaning up their manufacturing processes in the mid-'80s, producing higher quality motorcycles, flourishing on Wall Street. More and more people jumping on the bandwagon—stockbrokers, lawyers, the ever-faithful blue collar workers . . . and, in increasing numbers, police officers and fireman. Slowly, the dirty bikers became indistinguishable from the weekend warriors, who were also wearing jeans and black leather. Slowly the establishment assimilated the biker culture (or was it the other way around?)

Once it became impossible to differentiate the biker from the off duty fireman, or the off duty judge, the witch-hunt ended.

But please keep in mind that much of what follows was written in the years before that acceptance, years when bikers were truly discriminated against and hassled, and when there was genuine anger and resentment toward the establishment deeply ingrained in the biker culture.

Decades ago I wrote a column in "Iron Biker News" called "Mad As Hell." Each month I discussed a topic that was irritating me, or the biker community. In the connected world of the internet we would call it "rants."

I always had fun writing these. Sometimes the articles were antagonistic . . . sometimes innocently, sometimes intentionally, and I always loved the feedback I got from readers. In the early years it was via snailmail or in person at biker events, in the later years it was mostly via email.

Sometimes the readers agreed with me, sometimes they disagreed, vehemently. But it was always in the right spirit . . . we were, after all, a community. And all said and done, there is still a much stronger bond with a fellow biker, even one with whom you disagree, than with anyone out of the community.

Pilgrimage to Daytona, or, Where Have All The Bikers Gone?

Iron Biker News, November 1996

Every year Bob Steel (our publisher) asks me to go to Daytona with him. He loves the place—he's been going to Bike Week religiously for over a decade, and has gone to Biketoberfest since it began. He doesn't rave about the place, but he really doesn't need to—going to the same place for vacation every year speaks for itself.

He told me it's *the* place for bikers. So we set a departure date a week ahead of Biketoberfest—unlike March Bike Week this could be exactly what we like to do, a vacation where we could ride every day from the day we pull out of our driveway till the day we return. After all, in October, except for some unseasonable weather somewhere, you can still ride very comfortably in all 48 contiguous states.

So day one I rode the 300 miles over to Bob's. On the second and third days we did the other 900 miles. Now I'm not going to bore you with the road trip details, but I will pass along two things. First, I-95 is one seriously boooorrrrring road—900 miles of nothing at all. Second, we only passed two other bikes headed to Daytona the entire trip.

Let me clarify that—we only passed two other bikes that were being ridden. First though we passed a van, one of those custom ones that has a captain's chair for the driver and flared wheelwells and is always being driven around by someone so obese they look like they need an elevator to get in and out—and behind the Jabba-the-Hut Mobile was a trailer with not one, but two, motorcycles. Not just motorcycles, but touring motorcycles (Gold Wings). Now, I don't want to be too critical, but what do you need a touring motorcycle (or in this case two) for if you're going to drag it down the interstate behind your blubbermobile?

Since, as happens on interstates, we kept passing this same guy over and over; I had a lot of time to wonder about it and reached the (mistaken) conclusion that these Honda people don't ride their bikes like we Harley people do. By the time we reached Daytona we had passed about 18 other bikes, all Harleys, on trailers (OK, we did pass two Harleys being ridden). Now I was really curious—first of all how come we didn't see more bikes, and how come all the ones we saw were on trailers? Well, obviously, these must all be show bikes (even though they didn't appear any nicer than some non-show bikes Bob and I own, and ride).

But what really baffled me was—where were all the bikers we should have seen riding down? Was this a repeat of my first trip to Sturgis with Bob (when he got us there the wrong week)?

When we checked into the motel there were two other guys there, both with pretty righteous shovels, that came down in a van from NJ with the bikes in the back. Down at the other end of the lot was a guy cleaning his Delaware-tagged Ultra-Glide, obviously removing his thousand miles of road dirt—well it was a thousand miles of road dirt, the kind your bike gets from being trailered. So far the only people who rode were me and Bob.

The next day more people from NJ, Delaware and Pennsy pulled in (we stayed at a place popular with folks from there)—every bike came in a trailer or a truck, even the dressers all outfitted for touring.

Next day three guys from South Carolina rode in. When I asked them about their ride, the said, "Oh no, we didn't raaad, we unloaded the bikes across the street."

It keeps getting worse—then the guys from Florida pulled in, with their bikes in the back of their truck. So now, finally, the motel is sold out, all 60 rooms—from what we can see the only people that rode to this motel was us, and two other couples (an NJ police officer and wife on an FLH, and a 65 year old couple from Maryland). In all fairness though, some folks brought along their kids, and some other folks made Daytona an extension of a family-type vacation at Disneyworld, so it was easy to understand some folks not riding. But most of the folks who pulled their bikes in had themselves, an old lady, and a small bag with toothpaste and clean skivvies.

Anyway—nobody else in the entire motel rode to it, even though in the parking lot, in addition to the Rigids, Softails, FXRs, Lowriders, there were also FLHs, FLTs, FLTCUs, FLHCUs, and these bikes had bags, tourpacks, radios, fairings, etc. So obviously I was in a motel of "biker/trailerers," and the people who rode were elsewhere in town (wrong again).

I started (subconsciously at first) noticing which bikes weren't ridden in—obviously the Ness, Doss, Kennedy type show bikes were brought on trailers, as were the V8 Boss Hoss's, and the longbikes, and the . . . . OK, so it was impossible to figure out what was trailered, how about what wasn't—determined by one (or all) of—high odometer readings, clothing and other stuff all over the bike, bulging saddlebags, bikes that were clean and well maintained with the exception that the leading edges that hit the wind (like the front edges of mirrors) had the paint or plating worn off, etc. Our not-too-scientific research revealed that only a small percentage of bikes actually got ridden, and it didn't seem to matter what type of bikes they were.

Seems there's only a small percentage of people who actually like to ride—and it almost doesn't matter what they own, they'd rather ride it than get there any other way. Sometimes they were on big touring bikes, Ultras and Wings—other times they were on bikes that were a lot tougher to travel on, FXRs, Softails, Crotchrockets, with throwover saddlebags, tankbags, bungee cords, etc. The one thing they all had in common was—the best part of the trip was . . . . .the trip.

I spoke with some of the people who brought their bikes on trailers about why they didn't ride. One very seasoned looking couple who both rode (she a shovel, he a softail) told me that in their truck they have air conditioning and TV—now why would you need air in October, and if you want to watch TV maybe you should stay home on your sofa. Somebody else told me they wanted to get there fast—you mean your car can get there faster than your bike? Two other people told me that they had touring bikes but didn't want to ride those bikes, so they trailered their sportier bikes—OK, so why do you have a touring bike? But the one that took the cake was the guy who trailered his UltraGlide, cleaned it for hours after he arrived, hours every day, and couldn't have possibly ridden 50 miles the whole week—it seems 10 years ago on the way back from Bike Week he hit snow in Maryland. OK, I don't like to ride in the snow either, but guess what, it's the frigging second week of October—does it ever snow in Maryland in October?

When we were packing to leave I saw one of the guys from South Carolina (a six-hour ride) who trailered his bike. He asked me when we were leaving and how long it would take. When I told him it was about an 1,100 mile ride, his jaw dropped and he said "You're gonna raaaad? You're gonna *raaaad!!??*" You would have thought I said I was going to sprout wings and fly.

When Bob and I visited Daytona H-D we saw the new FLH Springer bike, kind of an early fifties looking bike with a springer and fringe and other equally useful stuff. The literature told us that The Motor Company designed this bike for "High Profile Cruising" (meaning driving slow down Main Street so other people can see you).

We decided we're going to release the "next generation" of bikes before The Motor Company does—we're building bikes for "High Profile Parking." These bikes will have the latest in paintjobs and chrome, but they won't have any stuff that's unnecessary to the high profile lifestyle—stuff like electrical systems, pistons, cams, wheel bearings, etc. (and an added benefit is it doesn't need any maintenance or repair, ever). You can load this bike on your trailer (it's pretty light), unload it on Main Street, chain it to a pole, and every night sit on it while you drink a beer and puff on your Havana cigar—then, you don't even need to take it home; you just put it in the storage bin at your condo down at Ponce's Inlet or West Palm. This way you can fly down each year, and as long as you arrange it with us in advance, just show up on Main Street where we'll have your bike pre-parked and waiting for you—any takers?

Sometime in the '80s certain folks in the biker community began to feel the lifestyle was being invaded by non-bikers who wanted in. People with disposable income buying new better-than-ever Harleys, donning distressed leather jackets, and posing as seasoned riders. It seemed there was always someone preaching about who is, or is not, a "biker."...and I was sick of hearing it. —Stu, 2014

Any *Bikers* Out There?

Iron Biker News, October 1997

Last week I was talking to a friend about the mass walkout of the editorial staff at "Iron Horse," lamenting the demise of a magazine I find very entertaining—"the last biker magazine," as my friend put it. Another guy I ride with said he thought IH was the only "hard-core" bike magazine left.

I started thinking about something that I had (intentionally) forgotten about years ago—the labeling of people, or groups, as "hard-core," "bikers," "citizens," etc. OK, so there are some labels that accurately describe a person's role—if someone tells you they're a doctor, this better mean they attended medical school, interned, were board certified, etc.—if someone says they're an attorney this means they've earned their LLD and passed the bar exam.

But what is a "biker"? Generally, this brings to mind the stereotypical image of a Marlon Brando/Wild One type—chip-on-the-shoulder rebel-without-a-cause, jeans, leather jacket, t-shirt, tats, Harley (I know, Brando rode a Triumph), engineer boots, etc. It seems a lot of people aspire to this image—especially new riders who seem to want to prove they've been riding longer than they actually have, know everything there is to know about bikes, riding and the "lifestyle." How come so many wannabe and new riders aspire to be perceived that way? Is there something wrong with being a new guy on a bike?

I recently read an article called "Defining Bikerdom" by Vulture, in the new on-line version of "The Horse." I don't know Vulture, nor do I remember reading anything of his before—but here are a few excerpts from his article:

- He says, "Numero Uno on my list of things that makes a biker a "biker" is an undying devotion to the Harley-Davidson V-twin powered motorcycle."

- He also says, "The rule is, bikers ride Harley-Davidsons, motorcyclists ride something else."

- Then later in the article "So, have I ever owned a japbike? Yep, sure have . . ."

So here we've got a guy, who labels himself a biker and sets himself up in his article as an "expert" who can tell the rest of us about bikers. He defines being a biker as an "undying devotion to the Harley-Davidson V-twin powered motorcycle." Then somehow, even though he admits his devotion died long enough to own a "japbike," he makes an exception of himself. In other words—he can ride a non-Harley and still claim to be a biker, but nobody else can. After all—there's a rule, which I guess we now need to modify to read "Bikers ride Harley-Davidsons, motorcyclists ride something else—except Vulture cause he wrote the rule." Don't you just love people who have the nerve to tell you how to live, even though they don't do it themselves?

It reminds me of all the 19'50s parents who smoked but told us it would stunt our growth. Or Bill Clinton proclaiming his undying devotion to Hillary—"but Hillary, I was thinking of you the whole time" (but Harley, I was thinking of you every time I climbed on my Honda).

One of the reasons I was attracted to bikes (choppers) in the '60s, and one of the reasons I've never stopped riding, is that unlike the rest of the environment (work, school, family, etc.) motorcycling didn't have any authority figures or preachy types making up a bunch of rules. Now I find out that not only are there "rules," but "bikers" are making them up. Great—what next? Will the biker hall monitors report me to the assistant principal cause I forgot the chain on my wallet, and make me drive around in a cage for 45 minutes?

So—what exactly is a "biker"? Is it someone with long hair, a beard, tattoos, and a wallet on a chain? Or someone who rides his bike every day? Or someone who has a more serious interest in motorcycling than anything else? Or someone who rides a certain brand or style of bike? Or someone who reads certain magazines, wears certain clothing, and belongs to the Bros Club? Is it all of these people? Maybe it's none of them? Maybe it's like the commonly accepted "definition" of pornography—"you can't define it, but you know it when you see it." I'm not being sarcastic when I say—after 30 years on a bike, I don't know the definition of "biker."

Recently I saw a guy wearing a black T-shirt that said BIKER in big letters. I've also seen a bunch of shirts proclaiming "Bikers are. . . . . this or that," or "If you ain't a biker you ain't shit." Thank goodness all groups don't feel compelled to wear these kind of shirts—I think I'd get sick of seeing shirts like "If you ain't a Roto-Rooter man, you ain't shit," or "Psychoanalyst. If you have to ask, you wouldn't understand," or "Better living through litigation—love your local lawyer."

So here I am, writing for Iron *Biker*—it's not Iron *Motorcyclist*, or Iron *Rider*, or Iron *Gentleman*. OK, so I ride a Harley, and I average over 10,000 miles a year, and the only other bikes I've ever owned were in the '60s and they were BSA's and Triumphs . . . and I never owned anything but an American car . . . and the only hobby I have is motorcycles. Even so, I'll admit it—I don't know if I'm a biker . . . . nor do I care. As a matter of fact, now that we've got people making rules about being a biker—when you see me just think of me as a serious motorcyclist, who's too damned independent to want to be labeled anything that's got a bunch of rules made up by teachers, cops, generals, lawyers, politicians or self-appointed gurus.

At the time I wrote this I was just plain embarrassed by our behavior at public motorcycle runs. Over the years the behavior has improved, but last summer's incident in New York City, bikers beating a motorist, broadcast over and over on the news and the internet, once again terrified the public and set our image back six decades. We remain our own worst enemy; and yes, a few rotten apples can spoil it for everyone. —Stu, 2014

Improving Our Image????

Iron Biker News, July 1998

The other day our publisher, Bob Steel, was talking about "our image," and whether or not all the various Toy Runs, Charity Rides and other image-building stuff we've done over the last 10-12 years has actually done anything to improve it.

For you non-students of biker history, a lot of our image problems stem from Hollywood's bizarre depiction of bikers. Marlon Brando did a fine job of portraying a social misfit in "The Wild One," and he unwittingly created the biker stereotype that we still suffer from today. This was crystallized in numerous moronic biker flicks, in which budding stars like Bruce Dern, Peter Fonda, Willem Dafoe and Jack Nicholson continued to reinforce the stereotype by playing cretins whose only interests in life were rape, pillage and dope.

By the time we entered the 70's, the general public (and law enforcement) all had a jaded impression of what bikers were— unfortunately all too often they applied that impression to anyone on a motorcycle. It also seemed like they believed that there was an inverse relationship between cc's and IQ—the bigger your bike, the smaller your brain.

That stereotypical impression remained strong right through the eighties. The best evidence was the frequency of unwarranted stops by law enforcement. You know—riding at the speed limit on a legal bike, but still being stopped (mostly because it's a Harley, and you're with six other guys on Harleys). After all, you can't blame law enforcement—they've seen the same movies—they know that right there under the surface is that bubbling lava of biker personality waiting to erupt in drug abuse, booze, rape and murder, as always happens when six or eight bikers get together. After all—Brando and Dern and Fonda and Nicholson showed us—it must be true.

As we rode into the Nineties, some of the stereotypes were changing (or, at least the unprovoked traffic stops were subsiding). I believe this was primarily the result of three related factors:

1. Harley had re-engineered the bikes and now manufactured a product that was not only cool, it now ran pretty well and didn't leak all over the garage floor,

2. Baby-boomers had as a group moved into a more stable, affluent phase of life, and many who had not been able to afford an expensive motorcycle when younger, could now easily lay out $8-10,000 for a new, improved (and still very cool) Harley, and

3. The combination of those two factors converged with Harley's financial planning to create an American Success Story on Wall Street (further legitimizing H-D with the affluent stock-savvy public and driving Harley's sales even further). Suddenly, professionals were buying Hogs—the average income and age of buyers was increasing—it became well known that the demographic of H-D riders was changing. It was possible that under the helmet you'd find your dentist or lawyer. Chrome and black was becoming commonplace in the garages of doctors, architects, lawyers, etc.

So how about these events which some people believe have improved our image? Most major events (and this excludes mega-events like Daytona and Sturgis) fall into two categories—awareness-building and/or charitable.

Awareness-building events are just that—motorcycle awareness rides, POW/MIA awareness rides, etc. Most awareness rides draw an enormous turnout. Very often the public has no idea what exactly the ride is about—all they know is that they're stuck on the side of the street while a bunch of loud Harleys ride by. Usually the riding is accompanied by horn-blowing and the revving of engines . . . some riders making as much noise as humanly possible with drag pipes. Often riders are weaving in and out, and passing on both sides. Also it is common, regardless of the law in the particular state, that many riders will go helmetless, in violation of local laws (just to keep it straight so you don't flood me with letters about helmet laws—I personally am in favor of freedom of choice, and remove my helmet wherever local laws permit). It is my belief that these runs never do anything to improve our image—in fact, given the little slice the public sees, the general impression created is a reinforcement of the Brando stereotype.

Toy Runs and Charity Runs are even worse. All the negative behaviors the public sees at Awareness Runs also exist at Charity Events. Add to it the historically anemic financial results of these events. 3,000 bikers turn out, and manage to raise $5,000 dollars—well, button your shirt before your heart falls out. 3,000 people all on very expensive motorcycles, and they manage to raise something that amounts to less than $2 each. I'm not making this up—next time you go on a Charity Ride, demand an accounting—you will be embarrassed. Additionally, since some promoters have verbalized that these events are intended to "improve our image," it's become quite clear that the events are self-serving, and that the charity aspect is secondary—also embarrassing. So in addition to reinforcing the Brando stereotype, a Charity Ride often leads the public to believe we're cheap and self-centered.

Well Bob Steel, I submit to you that these events do not improve our image. That in fact they promote a negative image—that of rowdy, reckless, law-breaking, self-centered, penny-pinchers. One of the eastern cultures believes that "If you want to improve society, begin by improving yourself"; I believe that if we want to improve our collective image, we should each work on our personal image.

Incidentally, I do not now, nor did I ever, believe we should do anything at all about our image. I have spent my entire life becoming what I am today, and I'm OK with it. I don't ride to impress, or to aggravate, anyone. I don't really care what anyone thinks about me riding a motorcycle. If someone doesn't like my "image," that's their problem, not mine. While I will continue to ride in events that support causes I believe in, I will also continue to not ride in events whose primary goal is "improving our image."

Live to Ride, Ride to Live

Iron Biker News, March 1998

You've all seen the derby and timing covers that Harley makes—"Live to Ride, Ride to Live." Not only have you seen them, but you probably have one on your bike or in your garage.

I saw a statistic the other day on how many of the Live to Ride covers Harley sells. I forget the exact number, but what I do remember is that it was staggering—and that was just last year's number. Harley's been selling these covers for at least ten years. Assuming on average Harley has sold about 100,000 new bikes a year for the last ten years, and a good percentage of new bike owners buy the "Live to Ride" covers, and assuming that lots of folks that already own bikes also buy these covers, then there's a damn lot of these covers in circulation. Let's say, for sake of discussion, there are a million of these covers in circulation.

I believe in the sentiment "Live to Ride, Ride to Live." Anybody who's ever read my column knows that there's absolutely nothing more central to my life than riding my bike. No matter how up, or down, I may feel when I get on my bike there's no doubt I will feel better when I get off. I don't know why it's true, but I know that it is true—I live to ride.

Life is nothing but a series of choices. Will I get out of bed today, or hide under the covers? Will I shower and shave, or will I live like street people? Will I go to work, or will I be a wart on the ass of society? Will I take the car, or ride today?

Every day I open my front door and make a conscious decision—will I ride today? Then there's a couple more questions—is it snowing? Are the roads icy? Are there other dangerous conditions? Do I have too much stuff to carry for the bike? Do I need to pick up other people? Well, most days the answer to all those questions is "No"—and as long as the answer is no, then there's no reason that I shouldn't hop on my bike. No reason other than—"It's too much of a pain in the ass to take the bike—I'll just take the car. After all, it's kinda cold, and kinda damp, and kinda . . . whine, whine, snivel, snivel. . . . ."

Without writing another very long article on how to dress for year-round riding let me just say—with a modest investment in proper riding gear most of us in the 48 contiguous states can enjoy a twelve-month riding season. If you need to find year-round all-weather riding gear you can always check out your local Harley or BMW dealer, or you can go mail-order with RiderWearHouse (probably the premiere manufacturer of custom-fit all-weather gear. Their motto is "Work to Ride, Ride to Work.")

Here we are, having one of the mildest winters in recent memory—at least in the northeast. It's darn near spring, and we've hardly left fall behind. Most weeks have not only been tolerable for riding, most have actually had at least one or two dry, warm pleasant riding days. I've put thousands of miles on my bike this winter—the easiest riding winter I remember, ever.

What I don't understand is—with at least two spring-like days every week all winter, *where are YOU????* Where are all you people with the "Live to Ride" covers on your bikes—you're sure not on the roads. Is there some unwritten law that after Thanksgiving, even if it's 55 degrees, you're not allowed to ride your bike? Are your bikes already loaded on trailers for the long ride (snicker, snicker) to Daytona, and you're not allowed to ride here at home?

You can choose to lock up your bike for the winter, girlyman, or you can make another choice—when you look out your door in the morning remember, Carpe Diem! (Seize the day!) It's all about choices—Live to Ride.

Back in the '80s and '90s the average age of a Harley buyer was increasing by about eight years in every decade. Though the average age hasn't increased as rapidly in the last 10 years as it had prior, I would reiterate my point from 1998 . . . Harley-Davidson must find a way to appeal to younger buyers. Period.

—Stu, 2014

Are We Headed for the Same Fate as Women's Bodybuilding?

Iron Biker News, January 1998

Are we headed for the same relative obsolescence as Women's Bodybuilding?

So there I was, sitting in front of my TV last week, waiting for Paul McCartney to appear on the Oprah Show. I'd never watched Oprah before but, hey, when was the last time you saw a McCartney interview—maybe in the late '60s when they were trying to explain away John Lennon's "more popular than Jesus" comment? I felt a sense of déjà vu as I waited; once before in nineteen sixty-something I sat waiting for Ed Sullivan to introduce The Beatles. It's hard to believe I've been listening to this guy for over 30 years.

It's a funny thing, but it seems the things that interested me in the late sixties have become my life. Back then it was rock and roll music, sci-fi, cars and choppers. I was listening to the likes of Steppenwolf, The Moody Blues, The Band, Dylan, Simon and Garfunkel and The Beatles. I was messing with a '57 Chevy with a 301. I was following Star Trek and reading sci-fi books. And after a few brief forays with British bikes I was spending most of my time with a certain primo panhead that I had for about 6 years.

So what's changed?—not much. Did I "grow up" like my parents insisted I would, and did I put away those "childish things," and did I pursue the same life as the elders in my clan? Let's put it this way—now I have a much bigger sound system and even though I do occasionally crank up a bit of Mozart or Tchaikovsky it generally plays a steady stream of modern rock & roll, names like Dylan, Paul Simon, McCartney and Elvis (all who have released new cuts, or brand new previously unreleased gems). I'll admit it—I watch all the sci-fi on TV, and I love it— Babylon 5, Voyager, Deep Space 9, Outer Limits, Highlander. And bikes—so I don't have the old Pan anymore, but I have a very rideable Evo that I put lots of miles on each year.

So what does all this have to do with anything? Now here I am doing pretty much the same things as I did 10 years ago, 20 years ago, hell 30 years ago. Now about 10 years ago I read a blurb that the average age of a Harley buyer was 36 years old; yesterday I saw Harley's new figures that said the average buyer age in 1992 was 38, in '93 was 41, in '94 was 42 in '95 was 42 and in '96 was 43. In about 10 years, the average age of a Harley buyer got 8 years older!

When I read articles about things that may jeopardize the future of motorcycling (like health insurance exemptions and restrictions, unreasonable EPA policies, and rampant legislation to protect us from ourselves) I have a concern. But this concern wanes in comparison to the fear I feel when I read Harley's buyer demographic figures. If I had to give up all my interests but one, I'd keep the Harley (you notice I said "Harley," not "motorcycle"). Sure, I love motorcycles, but there's something absolutely unique about a Harley. There's a sense of peace, satisfaction and gratification that comes over me every time I ride my Harley. Does it have something to do with the look, the feel, the sound? I don't know, but I do know it's unique and I get that feeling from nothing else.

Has there ever been an extended period in the history of The Motor Company that with each passing year the average age of buyers went up a year? You don't need to do any research to get the answer, because if the answer were "yes" then H-D would have gone out of business. What will the average age of a buyer be in 2002? Will it be 48 (as the trend indicates)? Will it go up to 58 by 2012? See where I'm going with this?

Now in 1967 I wanted a new Hog in the worst way, but $1,500 was a fortune. So I was one of those mid-thirties guys who bought a new bike in the mid '80s. And since the mid '80s there's been a shitload of middle-aged guys who've bought damn near every machine H-D has built. A lot of middle aged guys have bought two or three bikes in the last 10 years.

Maybe my viewpoint is myopic, but it seems to me that in the '60s there were cops on hogs, old guys on new dressers, but the majority of guys on hogs were "kids" of 18 to 25, who were after the speed and power that you could get from 1200 cc of H-D. Now I look around at people on Harleys and (don't get me wrong, I think it's great that as a generation there's so many of us graybeards still riding) I wonder where are those "kids," the young guys full of piss and vinegar that in the '60s were the mainstay of the Harley culture? They're sure not on Harleys in the '90s; hey, sure there's an occasional young guy, but for every young guy, there's 2 or 3 dozen middle aged guys.

Someone who I respect once speculated that "maybe H-D will always be a symbol of enduring coolness (like Levi's ever since James Dean)." I guess what I'm wondering is whether Harleys really are like Levi's, cool to people of all ages—or are they just cool to the generation that grew up in the '50s and '60s? If that's the case it'll be sad to see H-Ds fade into the semi-oblivion of chess or female bodybuilding. Remember how popular chess was in the Bobby Fischer years or female bodybuilding was in the Arnold and Rachel MacLish years—now chess is again in the hands of the nerds and female bodybuilding has faded into the woodwork.

It's entirely possible that the Harley culture could simply evaporate as we (as a generation) become more focused on the challenges of becoming senior citizens. I really don't want to see one of the best pieces of American life and culture become a piece of history, but I'm convinced if we don't find a way to attract (lots of) young people to our culture then this is just what will happen.

Any *YUPPIES* Out There?

Iron Biker News, November 1997

L ast month I was struggling with that age-old question "What (or who) is a biker?" I got a number of interesting letters—some gave me their view, others wrote to say they've also wondered the same thing.

In the meanwhile I read one of last months' Letters to the Editor which we published. Maybe you read it—it was from "Pappy." Pappy wrote to comment on what he felt was the disappearance of all the good biker people, who've now been replaced in the motorcycle world with a rich yuppies. He also said in his letter to Tom McTamney, our Editor, "Be careful Tom, you make too much money you might wake up someday a Yuppie and not even realize it."

So that got me thinking—"What is a yuppie?" I thought I knew—I thought a yuppie was a *Young Urban Professional.*

Now I know Tom (and so does Pappy):

- Young? Well, he just hit the half-century milestone. Maybe still young to some folks (Bob Hope, Art Linkletter, Ronald Reagan), but not to most.
- Urban? Last I knew, he lived just outside Landisville, NJ (go ahead, try to find it on the map)—one of the least urban places east of the Mississippi.
- Professional? He spends his time working on this paper, and building and repairing motorcycles. Not a doctor, lawyer, architect, etc.

So when Pappy said "yuppie" I knew that he didn't mean Young Urban Professional—that's not something you just become by making money. You need to be a certain age, live in a certain place, and be in a profession (I have two kids in college—I have absolutely no problem with my kids finding a profession they love, living in a city they like, etc.—by definition they'd then be yuppies).

But what Pappy meant (I think) was something very different. I've noticed the term loosely applied in the last couple years to a group of people I would define as "Have accumulated a bunch of high-profile stuff (BMW's, jetskis, flashy houses), have developed a certain look (pseudo-Ivy League), and put on certain airs (think they're better than a lot of other people)." In the '50s and '60s these were the people that had to project a certain image by "Keeping up with the Joneses."

The thing is—for the most part these people are not, by definition, yuppies. They may be a bunch of arrogant, despicable little phonies—who love to rub your nose in "look at what I have"—but we've always had that type of showoff in the world. *And*, they're not yuppies—actually I don't think there's a damn thing wrong with being, a real, live, young urban professional. So why don't we start calling an asshole an asshole, and stop giving a black eye to the (mostly) innocent yups.

And, if you need to label people, here's a few more for you:

Yuppies	Young urban professionals
Grumpies	Grim ruthless upwardly mobile professionals
Slumpies	Slowly losing upward mobility professionals
Farts	Fathers against rowdy teenagers
Shut Ins	Stay-at-home, unadventuresome traditionalists immobilized by non-safe sex
Swines	Students wildly indignant about nearly everything
Twerps	Those who enjoy routinely protesting something
Iacocca	I Am Chairman Of Chrysler Corporation Of America

Then there's the people we know:

Rubs	Rich urban bikers
Dummies	Downwardly mobile motorcyclists
Sitcom	Single income, two children, one motorcycle
Slobs	Sleazy lecherous old bikers
Snobs	Sensitive new-age bikers
Woofers	Well off, over fifty evo riders
Yummies	Young urban motorcycle mamas
Mommies	Much older motorcycle mamas

The world of biker magazines, circa 1995. I read a lot of magazines in those days, but didn't have a very high opinion of them. —Stu, 2014

Biker Mags

Iron Biker News, March 1997

Biker magazines, motorcycle magazines—I've been reading them for over 30 years. I sometimes wonder why I bother to buy them. Every month I read a pile of bike magazines, and every month I'm amazed at how bad most of them are. (Actually— this month I'm not quite Mad as Hell, more like "Aggravated as Hell").

I subscribe to three magazines, Iron Horse (there is no connection between IH and Iron Biker News—the similarity in names is a coincidence), Hot Bike and Motorcycle Consumer News. Then there are two that show up in my mailbox magically, HOG Tales and The Enthusiast, both from The Motor Company. But every month I also pick up a couple other mags over the counter to try to keep informed.

I want to know what's new from motorcycle manufacturers and aftermarket companies, I want to know what type of events are going on, I want to know what's new in the world of bikers rights, and I want to see pictures of what types of bikes other riders are building. Usually, I vary what I get. In the last year, in addition to my five monthly I've also read at least one issue of Easyriders, Outlaw Biker, Old Bike Journal, Biker, Walneck's, Hot Rod Bikes, Hot Rod Harleys, Indian, Rider, Cycle World, Streetfighters (Europe), Motorcycle International (England), AWOL (England) and some others whose names escape me.

I've usually got a pile of magazines to be read sitting in my living room. This pile usually covers—motorcycles, catalogs, computers, National Geographic (OK, so I just look at the pictures), science, electronics and some other stuff. There's always more than I can read. A couple times a month I go through the pile, read all the short articles and blurbs of interest, and turn down the corners of pages that have major articles to read at a later time. Because, like everybody today, I just don't have enough time, I must be very selective about what I read—I can't waste my time reading a bunch of inane crap.

When I start going through bike magazines, I look for very specific things—new products either me or my friends can use now or sometime, interesting pieces of "biker history" (which, to date, has not been chronicled very well), outstanding paintjobs that I want to remember, outstanding custom bikes or custom features that I may want to incorporate onto my bike someday, events that I may want to attend and anything else interesting that I come across.

It takes me about three minutes to "read" the two Motor Company mags—The Enthusiast has become a nothing more than a long glossy monthly ad that looks at H-D and its cycles through rose colored glasses; hey, if they want to do articles on the history of The Motor Company why not devote a few to the bumblefucks that ran H-D into the ground in the '60s and 70's, and to some of the other realities that H-D is not too proud of? HOG Tales—I haven't found a single article worth reading in the past two years. Every article is basically about what a great time it is to go to a HOG rally, or how Miss Mary Jo Grandmasky redeemed her otherwise barren life by buying the long awaited Willie G-designed FatMama motorcycle.

Then there's the magazine that we've all read from time to time (admit it); "read" is a stretch." I haven't "read" anything in Easyriders since the 70's, when they changed from a magazine that featured genuine ridden bikes, to a wannabe magazine featuring the un-rideable creations of "master builders" draped with Playboy centerfold rejects. Hey—the day they'll let me pick three of their feature bikes, and the owners'll hop on those bikes and follow me on a ten day five thousand mile trip, that's the day I'll change my opinion. The same goes for Biker (owned by Easyriders, and features all the stuff not quite good enough for ER), Hot Rod Bikes and Hot Rod Harleys. Until then, my opinion of these mags is that they feature "no-go showboats," and are written basically for wannabes, not riders.

Hot Bike is a magazine I really liked for a long time. It had good articles on do-it-yourself stuff the average backyard mechanic could handle—had bikes that were actually ridden—had no focus on "lifestyle," the focus was bikes. This magazine was originally Street Chopper, and was (is) owned by Tom McMullen, who you old-timers will remember was the man behind AEE Choppers in the '60s-70's. About two years ago McMullen's partner died, and they brought in new people to run the magazine. Howard Kelly, the ex-editor of Hot Rod Bikes, is now Hot Bikes editor; he has managed, in less than six months to bring this formerly great magazine down to the piss poor level of his last magazine. What do you expect from a showboat who wears a white leather jacket, rides a Buell, and can't let a single issue go out without at least a half dozen pictures of himself; the guy's a legend in his own mind. He and the rest of the staff have made dramatic moves to reformat the magazine and managed to completely forget its fine Street Chopper heritage (after decades, I'm not renewing my subscription).

Walnecks, Old Bike Journal, Cycle Shopper and a few others are basically classified ads, and they make no pretense of being anything else. I like these magazines—it' always interesting to see what's for sale, and how much it would cost to pick up an old Beezer or Triumph.

Cycle World, Rider and the other "establishment" magazines baffle my mind. The editorial policies are so anti-Harley, and the attitude pervades these magazines. If Harleys were as bad as every road test I've read in these magazines nobody would buy them. I buy these magazines a couple times a year, and get pissed off every time I do.

Motorcycle International and Streetfighters are two magazines published in the UK. They're hard to find (I have a friend who stops in the magazine store at the World Trade Center[1] and picks them up for me a couple times a year). I think I like these magazines cause I'm reading about another culture—bikes and biking are very different in Europe than here. Driving in Europe is really considered a privilege—it's much harder to get and maintain a license there. It's also a lot tougher to be riding a chopper, or a modified street bike of any kind. I love reading what they write about Harleys; remember, over there Harleys are priced damn near for the rich and famous. You can pick one up for about £22,000 (in dollars, that's $33,000).

Iron Horse is a magazine I like. It's written by real people, who really ride their bikes and who deal with the same BS you and I do every day. Often, I don't agree with their opinions, and sometimes I get downright mad—but, I respect these are real people and real opinions. IH doesn't carry ads from The Motor Company, CCI, or any of the other giants who could use their advertising clout to control editorial policy, and it's pretty clear that no one is controlling it. They say what's on their minds—and they have no respect for The Motor Company. There's a lot of IH that I'm not nuts about, or just plain not interested in—but this is the only magazine I get that regularly publishes articles worth reading. And, by the way, their feature bikes are not from "master builders"—they're usually street ridden city-type choppers. IH recently was sold to a different publisher—it's too early to tell whether or not they'll let the editorial policy alone (but you may have noticed already there are no more nekkid ladies in IH).

So out of the pile of magazines I get, there's only one that gets read regularly. Am I asking too much to find a magazine that has interesting editorials, street-ridden feature bikes, do-it-yourself

---

[1] I used to love the magazine store in the World Trade Center. It was on the floor called, I think, the Promenade, which was underground and was basically a big mall under the towers. The magazine store had stuff from around the world, and since the collapse I have never again found a store with the selection of international motorcycle magazines that I used to find at the World Trade Center.

articles for backyard mechanics, touring features that focus on do-able trips, a street and touring new products section, and an occasional nice looking old lady draped over a feature bike? Either I'm asking too much, or I've been looking in the wrong places for thirty years—if you know of anything worth reading every month give me a call (at Iron Biker).

The Hawk is Upon Us (Again)

Iron Biker News, December 1997

It's 7 AM—I look out the window. It's gray—I see the wind rustling the leaves—there's my neighbor walking her dog, and she's got a scarf wrapped around her neck up to her ears—my other neighbor's car is sitting in the driveway, idling, obviously running to get the heat on before he heads to work. Yep, the dreaded Hawk is upon us again.

I walk into my garage (attached) in my bare feet. Man, the floor's cold. My bike's sitting there, chrome glistening, paint shiny, ready to go. I put my hand on the gas cap—it's like grabbing an ice cube. Sheeeet—what happened to the warm, friendly days of summer—it seems as though it was just April, and now it's over.

The thought of firing up the bike, and heading out into the grayness of early winter certainly isn't as inviting as a summer ride. Hey, if it was summer, I'd hop on the bike and head over to the c-store for a cup of coffee—but is it worth putting on all those frigging clothes for a three minute spin? Nah—back into the house for a cup of my own coffee.

Time for work—my friend and I are opening a new bike shop, and I've got to go over to meet a contractor. It's about 10 miles, and I need to take drawings, a briefcase, and a bunch of other stuff. It's "warmed up" outside now—it's 38 degrees. I'm very tempted to take the car but—

I put on my flannel-lined jeans and a sweatshirt. About 10 years ago I got one of these H-D winter riding suits (it looks like a black snowmobile suit)—I slip it over my clothes and head into the garage. By the time I tie everything on the bike and get it started I'm sweating—*man, I hate winter*. And to make matters worse, my bike runs like crap till it warms up in the winter—man, this sucks.

Well, at least there's not ice or gravel/sand/salt on the roads yet—but man, there's an awful lot of folks who don't rake their leaves, and those suckers are as slippery as ice.

I get about halfway to work, and I'm almost on time. I'm pretty warm and comfy even though I've got on gloves and a faceshield, both which I hate to wear. The bike's finally warmed up, and feelin good like a Harley should—so I crank out 2nd, 3rd and 4th gear, slip it into 5th and settle in at 70 mph. I can feel the wind, but not the cold—I can hear my Porker Pipes, a little muffled with the face shield, but still sounding good. The couple motorists who notice me have that—"Hey, bikes are supposed to be in the garage for the winter" look.

Here comes my exit, and I've got about two minutes til I'm supposed to meet the contractor. Man, my bike sounds good—ah man, f--- it. So I crank it up and blast past the exit—ten miles, and two more exits down the road I get off, do a u-bee, and come back to my meeting. "I'm really sorry I'm late man, but I had some trouble gettin goin this morning."

Man, I hate winter—but I sure do love to ride.

Around the beginning of the new millennium, Harley-Davidson released a line of high-tech winter riding gear, black of course. And shortly after, heated gear. It caught on slowly, but now I do see some Harley riders on the road year-round. —Stu, 2014

A Chill in the Air

Iron Biker News, November 1998

The inevitable—shorter days, leaves falling, Thanksgiving—once again. And once again the end of the "riding season."

This year my perception is a little different. This year I spend all my time in a motorcycle dealership. Every day I see people on their bikes. Or people who are looking to buy bikes. So it seems like (at least in my little world) everybody's riding.

About a week ago I started to make a conscious effort to observe the world around me, especially when I'm away from the dealership. And once again, at this time of year, I'm seeing the inevitable—the bulk of riders in my area parking their bikes for the winter.

Suddenly, there's no one to wave to. There's no groups of four, five, six riders passing on Sundays. There's no bikes parked on Main Street or in the mall. And once again, I don't understand.

The brisk fall air is never better than from a Harley. The world never seems clearer or crisper. Truth is—I enjoy fall riding even more than summer.

This year I'm spending my Sunday's doing something that I haven't done in the last ten years—riding with the Polar Bears. No, these are not the guys who jump in the ocean on New Year's Day; these are motorcyclists who enjoy cold weather riding. Every Sunday from the final week of October until Easter they designate a location (different each week) to ride to. Each Sunday there's a lunch at the location (typically chili, clam chowder and hamburgers).

There's only one reason to ride to the Polar Bears—to spend a few hours with other riders who enjoy year round riding.

There's two things about the Polar Bears that surprise me (and this hasn't changed in the ten years since I last did this). The number of riders willing to go out in the winter is unbelievable—there are hundreds who show up every Sunday. And the percentage who ride Harleys is underwhelming.

I'm not sure exactly what the percentage of Harley ownership is in my area but, for the last thirty years, I wave to every rider I pass. So I tend to notice who's riding. My absolutely unofficial, unaudited count tells me that during warm weather, on Sundays, there are more Harleys on the road in my area than any other brand, and than all other brands combined.

So how come when I go to Polar Bears there is an embarrassing turnout of Harleys. How come I'm surrounded by BMW's with Hippo Hands—by Gold Wing riders with electric vests—by Kawasaki riders in snowmobile suits? Are the riders of BMW's, Hondas and Yamahas hardier, more impervious to cold, or more dedicated to riding, than Harley riders?

Actually, if you were planning to ride a bike less, why would anyone spend more (on a Harley)? Hard to understand.

Of course, in the middle of the winter electric vests, HippoHands, thermal suits, etc. are the norm for riding. Which brings up my theory that some people enjoy looking cool, more than they enjoy riding. It's a lot tougher to look cool in December than July—after all, unless you're really into cold it's impossible to sport jeans and a T-shirt. Once it gets real cold, a leather jacket and chaps just doesn't cut it.

I wear a riding suit. My wife thinks I look like a geek—or at least a man from Mars. Sometimes people do a double-take when I walk into a restaurant. Do I care? Cut me a break—if wearing a high-tech riding suit makes the difference between riding and driving I'll take the geeky riding suit any time.

To answer the question that I'm asked every winter—aren't you cold? The answer is *no*—if I was freezing I wouldn't do it. It's simply not that hard to stay comfortable if you use the right clothing.

Winter riding gear is not going to win you any fashion awards. Nor are you going to pick up any chicks when you're dressed like the Michelin man. But you will be able to enjoy riding your bike.

Now that you've spent ?? thousands of dollars on your bike, go spend a couple hundred more to get yourself set for the winter. For winter gear visit your local BMW dealer, Harley dealer or ski shop — or go to all three to get a combination of the stuff you need. If you can get in one decent riding day a week all winter I guarantee you it will make the winter seem shorter, more enjoyable and will do an awful lot to prevent the winter doldrums and cabin fever.

Distressed

Iron Biker News, February 1997

Yesterday I went through an annual ritual—cleaning and re-oiling my leathers. If you've read my columns over the last couple years, you already know I'm not a big proponent of leather. I just don't believe it's the ideal all-around wear-it-anytime-summer-or-winter answer to my riding needs, no matter how cool it looks, or no matter how cool those guys flying biplanes looked in WWI.

I think a lot of why we like leather is the look of military leather—primarily the WWI Bomber jackets and the German WWII full length coats. Of course, the military didn't wear these cause they looked cool—the military tries to buy things for functional reasons, and in the WW's leather was the highest tech fabric of the day. It was durable, flexible, (sort of) windproof, (sort of) waterproof, and compared to other alternatives was far superior.

I do think there's a place for leather, and I actually have two. One is a riding jacket, which I use in the spring and fall, and is a whole lot better looking than all my other riding gear—the other is a leather "duster" which I wear in the winter and in severe storms (rain, hurricane, etc.) all year. It is the best severe weather coat I've ever owned.

To keep the leather in good condition, every year I "oil" it. I use Neatsfoot Oil (some folks use Mink Oil); you just wipe it on, and over the next 24-36 hours it gets soaked into the leather. This replaces the natural oils (which are being lost cause the cow it came from is dead). It also gives the leather a nice, new sheen.

This takes me about three hours a year (you never realize how big a duster is until you've oiled every inch of one). I'm pretty sure that if I take care of my leathers like this, they'll last me a long time, maybe twenty years. *And,* they'll look pretty good. So what am I mad about?

I opened the new clothing catalog of a certain motor company. They've got a lot of leather; in particular though I noticed two jackets. The first is called (as though a jacket needs a name) a Billings Jacket and it's made of "Distressed brown cowhide with a used look and a rough feel," and the second is a Motorad Jacket which is a "Bomber style jacket in dry-milled distressed leather." So then I went to the clothing catalog of a certain major motorcycle magazine, and they have something called a Touring Jacket made of "antiqued cowhide." These jackets sell for $355, $350 and $429 respectively.

These fancy, expensive jackets are made to look *old*. The seams are all worn out looking, and the leather has that old unhealthy look that leather gets. So why am I spending an afternoon each fall oiling my leathers when other people are buying leather that has an intentionally worn out look? You can't blame the companies selling this stuff—there are, obviously, buyers. But who are these buyers, and why do they want to buy old looking clothes??

Remember the scheme Bob and I cooked up to sell "High Profile Parking" bikes? This was right after we got back from Biketoberfest, and had noticed that a huge percentage of bikes got to Daytona on trailers. This was also after we saw the latest Motor Company abomination, the FLH Springer (a '50s looking bike—springer front end, fringe, cream-colored paint, etc.) which was designed for "High Profile Cruising." This means riding only where other people can see you—like Main Street at 15 mph. So we figured we'd quantum-leap The Motor Company and release the logical next generation bike—a bike designed for "High Profile Parking." This is a bike you just park on Main Street and sit on—you don't need to do any maintenance—you don't need to be bothered with all that nasty riding stuff—you just have a couple flunkies (Bob and I) set up your bike on a choice spot ahead of time so you can show up and be an instant genuine Bro.

Well, here's Phase II. For all you guys who are buying genuine distressed leather, we're gonna help you be bikers through and through, not just on the surface. We'll sell you our old socks and skivvies, which have been broken in by genuine motorcyclists; please make sure to specify whether you want them washed or unwashed (unwashed is the direct shortcut to authenticity).

And then there's the second reason I'm Mad as Hell about leather. My son is graduating school and going out into the real world, so we thought a good thing to buy him was a suit (you know, for job interviews). So we went down to the Department Store to get a suit for my 6'4" son with a 32" waist. I was of course worried that they wouldn't have anything to fit a real tall thin kid—but lo and behold, they had every size suit from a 34 Short to a 52 Long. We had no trouble finding him a 38 Long that fit like a glove (not OJ's), and it cost $89. Eighty-nine bucks for a whole suit in a perfect size.

So how come these same big companies that sell distressed leather to distressed individuals, and get about $400, can't even offer them in sizes? I don't know about you, but I'm too big for a Medium, and too small for a Large. If I wanted to buy an $89 suit, I'd be able to get a 42 Long which would fit well; but if I buy one of these $400 jackets my choice is either wearing something I look like I outgrew when I was 16, or wearing something that looks like it was handed down by Uncle Fred. Hey, if I buy a $400 jacket I want it to fit right, and for that kind of money it should fit right and look good.

Have we all forgotten that until about 10 years ago leather jackets came in sizes, just like suits and overcoats (and last I looked both Brooks and Hein Gericke still had all their jackets available in real sizes). So how come these other behemoths of the biker world can get away with a "four sizes fit all" approach? Their motivation is obvious; producing and maintaining inventories of four sizes is cheaper than maintaining forty two sizes—and guess what, they don't have to pass the savings on to you, you'll pay the same price! (If you don't believe me, go price Brooks or Hein Gericke—you'll find they're no more expensive).

I'm not mad at them—there's a sucker born every minute, and they're just exploiting it. I'm mad at the folks who, like sheep, just go along. Next time you need a leather go to your authorized outlet, tell them you want that 44 Short—when they try to stuff you into an "L" tell them to stick it where the sun don't shine, then go buy yourself a jacket that fits. The only thing those bozos will ever understand is the sound of feet, a lot of feet, walking out the door without having left behind hundreds of hard-earned dollars for a one-size-fits-all coat.

A Good Day!

Stu Segal's LiveJournal Blog, December 2007

First, we had no fall—then winter started early about a month ago, and we've had either bitter cold or some kind of frozen precipitation for maybe four weeks. Add to that, I've been a bit under the weather since our return from the Yokohama Worldcon—which means I've hardly been on a bike since August.

Well today it was 45 degrees and sunny, so I decided Rashmika's Buell needed to be ridden since it's been sitting for a month. I took it out for about 45 minutes—felt so good that when I got home I fired up the Ducati and took that out. Well, that 150hp chuga-chuga V-twin felt so good that when I got home I fired up the BMW and took *that* out for a ride.

Amazing how good a ride on a motorcycle can make you feel. Amazing how much better *three* rides makes you feel. Frank Wu just posted his thoughts on how depressing winter is due to the lack of color—I agree, but offer the short-term cure . . . go for a ride!

Helmets have been an issue with motorcyclists for decades. I end this section with my 2014 thoughts, having now had 46 years since implementation of the helmet requirement in my state to think about this.

—Stu, 2014

Helmet?

Stu Segal, February 2014

I got my Driver's License in 1966, and immediately started riding a motorcycle for daily transportation. Having spoken with other people who rode, I took proper precautions for my safety—I wore a leather jacket (genuine military from my uncle!), heavy Wrangler jeans, or dungarees as we called them back then, and I always wore engineer boots. Oh, and sunglasses.

There was no New Jersey law requiring a helmet. And no one suggested it. Wearing a helmet on a motorcycle would be like wearing a helmet on a bicycle, or when skiing, which absolutely no one did in 1966.

The only people I ever saw wearing a motorcycle helmet were racers and police officers. Now the mounted police where I grew up had an entire badass look, part of which was the helmet—they wore white helmets with a badge on the front and a little peak to shade their eyes from the sun. Aviator sunglasses. Black leather jacket. Jodhpurs, like equestrians. High black leather boots that came all the way over the calf to just below the knee. And of course, they rode Harleys. They looked pretty intimidating . . . intentionally. And in that context, the helmet seemed quite appropriate.

Racers wore helmets for the obvious reason. There was a much higher incidence of accidents, and fatalities, in racing 50 years ago than there is today. Racing is still a risky business, but much riskier back then. The sanctioning authorities required helmets in all forms of racing.

But riding a motorcycle on the streets? Never saw a single person wearing a helmet, except the police. Not one, not anybody.

Then on New Year's Day, 1968 I was informed that New Jersey passed a "helmet law". Helmet? I had no helmet, I was not a cop, I was not a racer—where was I going to get a helmet? Today. Immediately. My bike was my transportation.

I looked where I looked for everything, in the garage, and found two helmets. There was a beat up football helmet; this was not my first choice, though some of my friends wound up wearing football helmets. And there was my dad's WWII USMC tank helmet. Have you ever seen a WWII tank helmet? Looks like an upside-down soup bowl, olive drab, with a grid of holes drilled all over every inch of it (the cockpit of Sherman tanks were so hot that if the helmet weren't ventilated the crewman would have a cooked brain). Pretty ridiculous, but the only helmet I had.

The other law that went into effect the same day was a motorcycle inspection requirement. Now, suddenly and unexpectedly, motorcycles would undergo the same scrutiny as cars and trucks. I went to my local police department to read the new motorcycle inspection regulations; it was obvious to me that in its current configuration my Harley chopper would not pass inspection, but it was equally obvious that with some minor modifications the bike would conform.

None of the modifications were difficult, just a little time-consuming. Handlebar height—the highest point of the handlebars could not be any more than 12 inches above the seat. I had apehangers, way above the limit—but a set of handlebars, new clutch and brake cables, and voilà, within the requirement. I had no front fender—but my friend had taken a fender off his stock bike, and a couple hours with a hack saw and drill refit his fender to my springer front end. I had straight shotgun pipes, also now illegal—but another buddy had removed the stock mufflers from his new Sportster, and they fit perfectly on my chopper.

It had taken me about a week in the evenings after work to modify the bike. But I was proud of the work, and confident it would pass inspection. So the next week I borrowed a "legal" helmet from my friend, and took a trip to the motor vehicle inspection station.

I waited, nervously, behind the cars, and when my turn came pulled up to the line. The inspector, who was dressed like a police officer, gave me a wide-eyed look when I pulled up; within seconds two of the other inspectors from further down the line came over. They were amazed—"You want us to inspect *this*?" Now *I* was amazed—what was the problem? Here I was on what I knew was a completely legal motorcycle, and the way they were acting you would've thought I pulled up in the Oscar Meyer Wienermobile.

Being young and naive, I didn't understand that it had nothing to do with motorcycle inspection. I was a long-haired 18-year-old, in a black leather jacket on a chopper. This was the era that authority, the establishment, was completely mistrustful of the youth of our country—college kids protesting the war, kids smoking grass and dropping acid, young people "dropping out"— besides being young and long haired, the ideal target for the little tin gods of the inspection station, I was clearly some kind of motorcycle degenerate.

Needless to say, the motorcycle did not pass inspection. I suppose what I could have done was sell the chopper, and get a nice stock motorcycle—perhaps a Triumph or BSA (a new Harley-Davidson was way out of reach financially). But that was not even an option, for two reasons—first, I loved choppers, and second, *no one* was going to make me stop riding *my* bike.

So I did what any of you would do. I went home, really pissed, and pulled an all-nighter—the next morning I blasted down the driveway with my straight-pipes and apehangers. And I rode that chopper with no inspection sticker for the next six years.

I *did* wear a helmet. Because even though I could get away with riding a chopper, there was no getting away with going helmetless. And I never did think much about wearing a helmet; there was no choice.

In the mid-80s I became a member of ABATE, American Bikers Aimed To Educate. ABATE's mission was repeal of helmet laws. Now, I really didn't have an issue with wearing a helmet, but I fully agreed with ABATE's position that this should be a matter of personal choice, not a matter of government control. We spent a lot of time and effort in New Jersey, and in other states—but in New Jersey there was simply no way we were ever going to have the law repealed.

As much as it should be a personal choice, the repeal of the law requires the support of the public, and many legislators. And we are not exactly the favorite special interest group of politicians; sure there are, and always have been, a few politicians who are friendly to bikers. But by and large the legislators, and the public, saw us as a bunch of loud, smelly, dirty bikers. It just wasn't going to happen.

There are of course benefits to wearing a helmet. The least obvious is actually the most compelling; the possibility that brain trauma could be reduced or eliminated in an accident. More obvious, at least in daily riding, is the reality that a decent helmet keeps the wind out of your eyes, the excessive noise out of your ears, and may also keep the sun out of your eyes. In winter, a helmet keeps your head warm.

I would like to think that, being a mature levelheaded person, I would wear a helmet even if the law were repealed. However, a few years back Rashmika and I went cross country—once we got west of Pennsylvania we never again rode in a state that had a helmet law. And guess what? West of Pennsylvania, we never wore helmets. Which sure does feel good in the blistering heat of the summer.

I will probably be compelled to wear a helmet every time I ride in New Jersey for the rest of my life; I accept that the helmet law isn't being repealed. Regardless, I continue to believe that wearing a helmet should be a personal choice, as should smoking, skydiving, wearing a seatbelt, taking drugs, and a thousand other activities that present risk. Is the government going to legislate safety in every aspect of our lives?

While I understand that left to our own devices we sometimes make poor choices, I would rather see an America with the freedom to make a poor choice, then an America where our safety has been legislated and our freedom of choice removed. If the law were changed today, I would continue to wear my helmet... but I would feel much better doing so knowing *I* made the decision.

the machines

Harley-Davidson quality issues, a never-ending topic of conversation. —Stu, 2014

To Harley or Not To Harley, That is the Question

Iron Biker News, September 1994

Bob Steel, who is my friend and oftentimes traveling companion, asked me to write a brief piece on our recent trip to Watkins Glen. This was a 3-day weekend trip of around 800 miles. It had all the necessary elements of being a great trip—about 50 miles of great sport riding down two-lane twisting offbeat paths through the Poconos, about a hundred miles down PA Route 6 (a road out of the '50s), and 3 days of 80+ degree weather. So what could be wrong?

On day two my 1986 FXRS, on which I have put 35,000 trouble-free miles, broke. Not a very big deal, but enough to get my attention. Some obscure part inside the transmission sidecover broke in half—diagnosed as simple metal fatigue which is the kind of thing that affects an 8 year old 35,000 mile machine. Being a realistic guy, I naturally think—"If the obscure whatchamacallit can disintegrate unexpectedly, what next?" And the stark reality that I own an aging bike which may no longer give me the type of uneventful service which I need if I'm going to have great vacations (vacations that are about riding, not fixing, my bike).

No problem, right? Admit that after 8 years a new ride is the ticket, and get the local dealer to place an order. Well, it's not that easy to give up an '86.

When I first started riding (late '60s) I couldn't afford a new H-D (as a matter of fact, I rode for 20 years before I bought a new bike). It didn't really matter though—

Harley was really building crap back then. The Harley and Davidson founders were dead, and the business was being milked by their moronic offspring who were drawing big paychecks and building bikes that leaked from every gasket. Worse yet, they didn't even care—they just shit all over their customers and laughed all the way to the bank. Ultimately their management deficiencies forced them to sell out to AMF (who made great bowling stuff, but knew nothing of bikes).

I bought my bike new in '86. Maybe you remember '86—it was a great year for Harley-Davidson. They had finally gotten rid of AMF (who had somehow managed to manufacture motorcycles of the same inferior quality as the prior owners). They had started to put the poor quality products behind them. They took the company public by offering their stock on the American Exchange. People from throughout the world of manufacturing were praising Harley's new engineering processes. They were selling more bikes, accessories, and stock in the company than they could supply. Since they were paying so much attention to things like continuous improvement and quality control, it was a great year to buy a Harley.

I believe in 1986-89 Harley hit their high point in producing high quality, low defects product. From what I see, they are now repeating their sins of the '50s. They are again manufacturing motorcycles with serious defects, and since there's so much demand for their bikes, they don't seem to really care (right back to shitting all over the customers).

Bob Steel (remember him, the guy that asked me to write a touring article) buys a new FLH type bike every 2-3 years. His logic is he can tour for a couple years on each bike—before it gets old, worn out, and starts breaking—and then he gets a new one. (Makes sense, right?) Three years ago after Bob got his brandy new FLH and did a little break in, he headed West (with less than a thousand miles on the bike); he got about 100 miles from home, and, *surprise!*, blew his transmission—it just plain came apart. (Bob never again trusted that bike.) This year Bob got a brand new Road King; again, with less than a thousand miles, *surprise!*, the bike caught fire—somebody at the factory forgot to put a necessary thrust washer under his ground cable, and the electricity found its own ground—right through his throttle cable housing to the gas tank.

So there you have my dilemma. Do I continue to ride my metal-fatiguing FXRS, or do I chance buying one of the new H-D "surprise" bikes. What do you readers think? Is history repeating itself—is H-D returning to the same manufacturing and customer attitudes that got them in so much trouble in the '60s and 70's—or is it just my imagination?

My Favorite Harley?

Iron Biker News, June 1998

I recently got a letter from a long time, faithful reader inquiring as to "my favorite Harley." He wasn't asking out of intellectual curiosity; he's planning to buy a new Harley, and was wondering what I prefer, given the amount of riding I do. Now, the obvious answer is—my favorite Harley is the one in my garage. But that's sort of the same as—"Where have you had the best ravioli (or pirogis, or kielbasa, or corned beef and cabbage, or whatever your ethnicity)"—the answer has to be "Mom's."

When I was a wild and crazy teenager the only one kind of H-D I really liked was a chopper. As long as the factory fenders and tank, the tins covering the forks, the exhaust system, the handlebars, the seat, speedometer, headlight, taillight, front wheel and front brake were all trashed, and replaced by a narrow front wheel, no brake or fender, apehangers, peanut or coffin tank, no speedo, chopped back fender, bates seat, straight pipes and sissy bar then it was okay.

Now I've become more mellow, and more appreciative of different styles of bikes. I like the old classic H-Ds, either 80" Flatheads or more modern Knuckleheads in rigid frames, and I like them in stock configuration or as choppers. I also like the more modern bikes—Panheads and Shovelheads, either in rigid frames or swingarms, either stock or custom. I like Evos, in all the various evo frames (Dyna, Softail, Swingarm FL, FXR), and in older or custom rigid frames.

But I also find that I like the H-Ds that other people tend not to. For instance, the FXRT was an FXR-based touring bike made in the eighties—most people think it's ugly; I personally think the looks of the bike is secondary to its function. In this case, a touring bike with all the amenities but 150 pounds lighter than the Sherman tank-like Ultra Glide. I also like the Tour Glide/Road Glide—you know, the funky looking FL with the frame mount fairing and dual headlights; again, to me the form is secondary to the function (a frame mounted fairing is simply superior to one mounted to the front end). FXR's are the same story—although the looks turned a lot of people off, this was the lightest, fastest, best handling of all the big twin frame configurations.

Then there's the more unusual. I like H-D ServiCars—I had a couple back in the sixties and seventies (and I wish I still did). How about XR's, KR's and VR's—yep, I like them too. Then there's Sportster's—I've never owned one, but I'd sure like to get my hands on a cafe racer. Buell's —I like them too.

How about other V-twins? Well, I especially like Vincents—the legendary 1000cc British V-twin that went out of production in the mid-fifties. I rode one in the late sixties—what an awesome motorcycle. Other V-twins? The Ducatis—the Monster and others—they're not very H-D looking with their 90 degree engines, but I also like them. Yamaha V-max (now I know a lot of folks will think this is blasphemous, but)—hey, a V-4 that can blow off any production car or motorcycle ever produced in a quarter mile, and can crank up to a legitimate 150+ mph from the factory—what's not to like?

How about the Valkyrie? Man, a 6 cylinder 6 carb 1500cc bike— the only thing wrong with it is that it wasn't built by Harley. And the new you-love-it-or-hate-it BMW cruiser—I wouldn't say I love it, but I do like it. I don't want to forget—I also love classic bikes— BMW, Triumph, Norton, BSA, Royal Enfield, Indian, Vincent, Ariel.

Are there any bikes I don't like? YES!! I don't like copies. This idea that you can copy a Harley, rename it, and claim it's as good as the original makes me sick. I've had, as I'm sure you have, crummy scummy people approach me on the streets of New York to sell me "Rolex Watches" or "Mont Blanc pens." Now both they and I know they're selling counterfeits, which I the only reason I can buy a "Rolex" for $15.

However, the companies trying to foist these copies on an unsuspecting and ignorant motorcycling public never exactly disclose the real difference between a Harley and a non-Harley copy. Take a look in the AMA Official Motorcycle Value Guide at the relative values of used Harleys vs. every other brand. I'm sure it won't surprise you to confirm that H-Ds command a much higher resale value than everything else. The one thing no one can copy (and somebody ought to let the large Asian manufacturers in on this) is the "brand," and the attributes both real and perceived that people ascribe to the brand—this brand is so strong that the vehicles actually appreciate in value.

Can you successfully copy a brand? I don't know. How many pretenders-to-the-throne have there been to brands like McDonalds, Coke, UPS and Corvette over the years? Some of McDonalds competition is actually very good—but on that rare occasion that I want a greasy breakfast, give me a genuine Egg McMuffin, not an impostor. Anyway—I'm ranting and raving because many of my motorcycling brethren (or would-be motorcycling brethren) are sucked in by impostors; in the end they lose money on the original purchase and eventually need to make a second purchase to get a genuine Harley.

But in answer to the original question, my favorite Harley is— *all* Harleys. But the truth is, with the exception of cheap copies, I love *all* motorcycles. And . . . if you happen to have a Vincent you want to part with, I have a parking space in my garage.

I got a lot of hate mail for this article, more than for anything I'd ever written for Iron Biker, from folks who just plain didn't understand.   —Stu, 2014

Springers, FXR's, and Bullet Taillights

Iron Biker News, March 1999

"Cadillac, Cadillac,
Long and dark—shiny and black.
Open up, your engines let em roar,
Tearin' up the highway like a big old dinosaur."

Bruce sang about them in "Cadillac Ranch"—if you're about my age the song conjures up images of maybe a '59 Eldorado. As long as a battleship, gleaming black, with the biggest fins and bullet taillights you've ever seen. Motoring down the highway like a roaring freight train, a 6,000 pound beast floating up and down on that suspension like only an old Cadillac can.

And there it is again on the new '99 Cadillac Eldorado brochure. Sure enough, right on the cover—a '59 Eldorado. And (believe it or not) in the centerfold of the Caddy brochure an Eldorado next to a Harley????

Sure seems like there's an obsession with nostalgia.

With Harley it seems to have started with the Heritage, and has become more and more perverse with each redesign. Next we got springers—then we got black springers—then we got fringe and tombstone taillights. Then we got wrinkle finish. Then FXRs. I'm afraid to wonder what's next.

Not that I have anything against the designs and styles that are our heritage and lineage—it's just that I believe in "continuous improvement." So when you have a design, and you improve upon it incrementally, you wind up with a better mousetrap—and it seems perverse to resurrect designs that are inherently inferior.

Hey, I owned a really great panhead in the sixties. It had a springer front end (chrome!), was on a '53 rigid frame, and had a rear juice brake (no front brake). Through the rose-colored glasses of my memory it was as cool as Fonda and Hopper's bikes, started on the first kick and my trusty steed never failed me. In reality it was a nasty beast like all '50s/'60s machines—the springer bounced uncontrollably, especially wedded to a rigid frame, it started when it wanted, it left its oily mark everywhere. I loved it, and compared to other vehicles of its era, it was pretty good.

But let's not kid ourselves; compared to today's technology it was a crude and inefficient. I'll take a pan over a knuck anytime, and an evo over a pan, and a twincam over an evo. I don't long for the vehicles of the good old days, and I really don't know why anyone does.

Hey, I like the '90s—color TV, 70 channels, CDs, microwaves, the internet, dishwashers, cell phones. I really don't want my old black and white TV that got 12 channels (all snowy). Nor do I long for my scratchy old records. And I definitely have no desire to ride any bike with a girder or springer front end again—ever. Nor do I want a bike without hydraulic rear suspension. Or no electric starter.

So what is this obsession with "nostalgia"? It's not just Harley. VW re-released the Beetle, and they're everywhere. Ford is bringing out a new version of the 2-seater Thunderbird next year. Mercedes is resurrecting the 300SL Gull Wing. Chrysler is working on a sedan-delivery.

Sure, the originals were cool, just like the Harley springer was 50 years ago, but who wants a 50 year old anything? Maybe for a novelty, or for a couple hours, but would you want to kick start your bike every day, or crank your car? Would you want to give up your twincam horsepower for the anemic power of a flathead?

Not me! As a matter of fact, I wish Harley would stop living in the past. All we seem to get from Harley is further proof that they can continually refine antiquated designs—so now we have a better dinosaur (but it's a dinosaur nonetheless).

Hey Harley—give me overhead cams, 4-valve heads, liquid cooling, more cylinders. If you want to stop making inefficient dinosaurs in favor of a new, efficient, non-V-twin powerplant that can compete with today's fastest, I'll be the first in line to get one.

In the meanwhile, I'll keep riding my antiquated-design 1999 Harley—cause all said and done, it's a Harley. And if you have to ask . . . . . .

Bullet Taillights, Part II

Iron Biker News, April 1999

I didn't really plan a Part II, but I got some interesting responses to last month's article: "You don't like old stuff, huh?" "That was a really anti-Harley article" etc.

I guess I failed to communicate my point—because I do like old stuff, and I'm not anti-Harley. Hey, there's nothing I like more than a clean pan or knuckle—or a rare Vincent or Brough. But the technology that made that Vincent great in its day, and can still be appreciated, is simply not the technology I want in a ''90s (or 2000) machine.

Harley-Davidson, and all the other major manufacturers are using the same platform—the internal combustion overhead valve engine. Nobody's using a rotary, or electric, or hydrogen. Although some people would like you to believe there's something different (better?) about a two cylinder V-twin with an offset crankpin, there simply is no basic difference. You can line the cylinders up (inline), put banks of cylinders at an angle (v), surround the crank with cylinders (rotary), lay banks of cylinders across from each other (opposed), etc. and you still have an internal combustion OHV engine. Sure, there may be some different performance characteristics, but the same basic engine nonetheless.

So what's my gripe about the current H-D design? The difference between the earliest OHV engines and todays finest is that over the years there have been many small improvements applied to the original design; the result of all these incremental improvements together is engines that are much more efficient (economical and/or powerful) than the original engines.

Interestingly, there haven't been any dramatic changes (quantum leaps) in usable engine design in a half century (by usable I mean able to be mass produced and marketed). An example of quantum leap improvement would be—

Maybe you remember recording tape in the '60s. Good quality sound could only be achieved on a big reel-to-reel tape deck, and it had to be running on a fast speed. Then someone invented Dolby, which removed the hiss from tape. This allowed tape to be run much slower, and still sound good. That led directly to the marketability of the cassette tape, which prior to Dolby had been un-usable as it sounded so bad. The development of Dolby, and of the cassette tape, are both incremental improvements—the end result, the cassette, although dramatically different from the predecessor reel-to-reel was, after all, still magnetic tape.

Then came the quantum leap—the CD. While most folks don't have a recordable CD, take note of how few of your friends are still listening (in their homes) to either records or tape. The CD is such a vast improvement that it nearly completely replaced all other forms of similar media.

Back to motorcycles, and my point. *No*—there has not been a usable quantum leap since the manufacturers all moved to overhead valve engines. OK, so Mazda tried the Wankel rotary— but it failed. And no one has been able to make electric work—or wind—or sun—or anything else. So we are all still using the overhead valve internal combustion engine—Harley, Honda, Ford, GM, Lamborghini, Kia—everybody.

My beef is with Harley's reluctance (refusal) to apply known incremental improvements. Things that would improve efficiency (horsepower, torque, mileage, etc.) or drivability (engine heat or handling). Now, (and hear me out before deciding I'm blasphemous) implementing any number of incremental improvements that are not today used by H-D, might require Harley stray from the known success formula of today (big heavy nostalgic V-twins). For instance, overhead cams, or maybe even dual overhead cams—or how about liquid cooling? These are changes that might lead to dramatic design change (and improved motorcycles)—but that change scares Harley, scares them that they might kill the goose that laid the golden egg.

Right now Harley sells all the bikes it builds. Forget for a minute the performance of the machines—regardless, all the bikes get sold. And this is primarily because the Harley—the look, the sound—has become a status symbol. Why change a good thing? After all, look at Harley's financial performance and that of its stock. Changing the basic design would be tantamount to Coca-Cola changing their formula—whoops! I forgot, Coke did change the formula. OK, they subsequently re-released the original formula as Coke Classic, but the new formula's doing OK too.

All I'm saying is how about building a modern Harley. Maybe four or six cylinders, liquid cooled, injected, dual overhead cam. Something that when I pull up to a red light next to a twenty three year old on a lime green Yamazuki I don't have to slither away, knowing that I have only half his horsepower. What I want is what I got when I bought my first Harley in the sixties—the biggest, fastest, most powerful machine on the road. Something that not only looks great, but will run circles around everything else on the road. Something that gives me the same feeling as my 1200 Panhead did in '67—the feeling you get when you know that when you twist the throttle, the only thing they'll see is your back tire pulling away.

Two years later, this is really Part III of "Springers, FXR's and Bullet Taillights."   —Stu, 2014

V-Rod

Iron Biker News, August 2001

About two years ago I wrote an article entitled "Springers, FXRs and Bullet Taillights," which was about the continuing trend of marketing retro-type products to a public that just couldn't get enough of things like the PT Cruiser, the VW Beetle, the Heritage and the upcoming Thunderbird.

My article focused on Harley's reluctance to move away from the tried and true 45-degree air-cooled V-twin which, by two years ago, was a 50 year old design. Sure, it incorporated 50 years of incremental improvements—and my comment was "All we seem to get from Harley is further proof that they can continually refine antiquated designs—so now we have a better dinosaur (but a dinosaur nonetheless)."

I went on to plead for DOHCs, liquid cooling, higher compression, etc., etc. "All I'm saying is how about building a modern Harley? Maybe liquid cooled, injected, dual overhead cam. Something that when I pull up to a red light next to a twenty three year old on a lime green Yamazuki I don't have to slither away, knowing that I have only half his horsepower. What I want is what I got when I bought my first Harley in the sixties—the biggest, fastest, most powerful machine on the road. Something that not only looks great, but will run circles around everything else on the road. Something that gives me the same feeling as my 1200 Panhead did in '67—the feeling you get when you know that when you twist the throttle, the only thing they'll see is your back tire pulling away."

This article seemed to push a lot of peoples' buttons; I got more hate mail than from any other article I've ever written. Some people said I was "anti-Harley"—they couldn't seem to understand that what I want is a bike that's fast, not just "fast for a Harley," a bike that handles well, not just "handles well for as Harley."

About a month ago Harley introduced the new V-Rod. It's a state of the art liquid cooled, 4-valve, DOHC, high compression engine in a dramatically styled bike. The fit and finish of the bike, which is capped off with anodized aluminum sheet metal says "high tech," but the dimensions and stance of the bike says "Harley"—so the end result is "High tech Harley." The engine, which is smaller displacement than the current "big twin" puts out a whopping 115hp – power unprecedented in Harley's 99 years of production motorcycles. Of course, it doesn't have the torque characteristics or the sound we all love—but what it has is performance.

Three months ago Honda ran ads for its' 1800cc VTX V-twin cruiser—proclaiming that it has "pistons larger than a Hemi" and the "world's most powerful cruiser." I don't suppose Honda, or anyone else, ever thought Harley would shrink the engine, and grow the performance (a very European approach). Who would have thought that H-D would go to Germany, France and Italy for design and production help?

I've seen interviews with all kinds of people from The Motor Company—from Willie G. (still acting like he's the savior of humanity, and damn near twisting his arm out of its' socket patting himself on the back) to obscure engineering geeks. I've seen at least six articles where spokespeople for Harley have said some form of "Well, it won't be for everyone" (as though they're afraid to offend the faithful) – I guess they'll get the same hate mail I did.

All I have to say is *Bravo Harley!* I was wrong—I thought your head was in the sand, but in fact you were more in touch with reality than I could have hoped. Let me reiterate what I said before—I couldn't care less if it's not an air-cooled V-twin, as long as it's a world-class competitor. I couldn't care less if it doesn't go "potato-potato" as long as it can hold its' own against the other brands.

I have had waning interest in riding my Harley (FLTRSEI Screamin' Eagle Road Glide) which, according to Harley, is the most powerful H-D ever built – in fact, it's an 800 lb. slug that can't get out of its' own way, handles like a truck, vibrates off any nut or bolt that's not Loctited, puts out enough engine heat to fry an egg. . . and certainly can't hold its' own against an S4 Monster, Hayabusa or K12RS. In a world of 130, 140, 150 HP Yamahas, BMWs and Suzukis, 70 HP Harleys just don't cut it. I don't know about you, but I'll have no regrets about taking my last ride on a dinosaur and throwing my leg over a piece of world-class technology.

I commend Harley for having the guts to step into the 21st century in style. I probably shouldn't ask for too much at once, but now—how about ABS, anti-dive and high speed aerodynamics so we can use that 140 mph speed?

Congratulations Harley, welcome to the future.

At the time I wrote this, Tom and I were considering adding these "British" bikes to our soon-to-open Harley dealership; we ultimately decided against it. These little Enfields are still produced, still inexpensive, and still fun. Triumph has come back in a big way and Norton is being produced in limited numbers.; the 21st century is really great for fans of British bikes. —Stu, 2014

British Invasion
Return of the Enfield

Iron Biker News, December 1996

B ack in the '60s I had some British bikes—a 650 BSA and a 650 Triumph. My buddy had a really cool 500 Royal Enfield, which he lowered, chopped the fenders, built a custom seat and sissy bar—it was righteous.

There weren't a whole lot of bikes or bikers back then, but guys who rode Hogs and Limeys all hung together—I guess we thought we were going to fend off the Japanese invasion. Beezers, Trumpets, Enfields, Snortin' Nortons—who would have ever thought they'd all go the way of Indian, Ace, Henderson and others?

But by the mid 70's they'd gone the same way as the British car industry—down the tubes. British bikes became a thing of the past. As I got older I forgot all the really aggravating things about Limey bikes (like the Lucas electrics) and developed a nostalgic longing for the Brit bikes; but alas, it was not to be. There were persistent rumors about a rebirth of British bikes, but they were about as credible as the rumors about Indian. (Yes, we know Triumph is in production again. They today build bikes which compete with the Japanese manufacturers for the "sportbike" market)

Enter Marty Scott, a New Zealander who lives near D.C. and is a British bike enthusiast. In the late '80s Marty learned that Royal Enfields were still being manufactured, in Madras, India, and were being sold in India, though not being exported to the U.S.

Royal Enfields in India???? (Well OK, not *Royal* Enfields, just Enfields). Seems that in 1954 the Indian government ordered 800 Enfield Bullets from England, for use on the Pakistani border. The Indian government ordered 800 more in '55, and 800 more in '56. This placed such a strain on the Enfield factory that they decided to open a factory in India and produce the bikes right there.

By 1956 a partner had been found, staff had been trained in England and a complete factory opened in Madras. This factory produced 1955 Enfield Bullets, 10,000 of them the first year. Every year since then (even though the original parent company went broke) they have produced over 10,000 bikes, never changing the design—the bikes made in '56, '66, '76, '86 and this year are all the same, *the 1955 Enfield Bullet!*

Soooo—in 1989 Marty stared working through the necessary DOT and EPA approvals to bring Enfields into the U.S. Five years, and countless gray hairs later, Marty won approval and in 1995 the first shipment of brand new 1955 Enfields arrived in the U.S.

We went to DC, met Marty and rode his Enfields. The 500cc bike retails for $3,995 ($4,395 for the Deluxe model with chrome gas tank). We brought all of the sophisticated equipment you would expect for a topnotch road test, worthy of publication in Car & Driver. We took the Iron Biker Kenworth rig, complete with the entire team of eight employees, chronometers, dynamometer, scales, altimeters, PC's, etc. (Actually Bob and I rode down, and brought all the essential equipment—a helmet). Seeing as we've never been in the business of doing road tests, we weren't constrained by needing to do a bunch of pretty meaningless objective tests (acceleration, braking distance, dry weight, etc.). We decided on a single criterion—do we like the bike?

Now through the day Marty repeatedly reminded us of the '50s manufacturing techniques, and how this is (in his words) "a tinkerer's bike." Actually, Marty's perspective helped us remember we weren't dealing here with the latest 16 valve DOHC monoshock, etc., etc.,—we were dealing with a 1955 motorcycle, something few of us have ridden in the last 40 years.

There were three bikes available to ride—a stock "test bike," a stock customer's bike (which had the handlebars and seat altered to handle the customer's 6'5" height), and Marty's personal slightly hopped-up bike.

First we went through the starting drill. This is a 500cc single, and it does not have electric start. So, for those of you who remember the BSA 441 Gold Stars (and similar bikes) this bike is equipped with a compression release, and the starting drill is the same (although the truth is, the stock bike is 6.5:1 compression, and if you have a mind to, you can kick it over without the compression release). All the bikes were a cinch to start. Part of the requirement for import to the U.S. is uniformity of controls (throttle, brakes, clutch), so everything is exactly where you'd expect it to be. (The factory fabricated a Rube Goldberg type of conversion to reverse the shifter and the rear brake, and Marty tells us that many owners have de-converted to gain a more positive feel to the controls, and a more "purist" look to the bike).

Now, Bob and I both ride Harleys, and rarely ride anything else—so we're used to big low-revving torquey engines. Neither of us had any trouble adapting (I just tried to remember that it was like my Geo Tracker—as long as you keep the revs up it hums along, but never, never expect to climb a hill in 4th gear from 2,000 rpm). The stock bikes rode well—for a 500cc single acceleration was good, handling was very nimble. The most evident reminder of the '50s technology was the brakes; I've become so accustomed to the positive feel of disc brakes that by comparison the drum brakes felt mushy and slow. The bikes were devoid of any rattles, shakes, clunks, etc. Now, we were on suburban roads (not a test track), and the stock bikes easily cranked up to 70 mph; they didn't have the stability of my 735 lb. FLT at that speed, but—hey, what do you expect?

Marty's personal bike was a lot of fun. He'd made a modest investment in increasing the bike's performance (upped the compression, changed the carb, changed the muffler). He also changed his brakes and shifter back to the original configuration, and while my brain kept telling my feet what to do, my feet kept doing what they had the last 30 years—so, even though every shift took me 20 seconds, the bike was fun to ride. The power band was much wider than stock, and the bike was pretty peppy.

Overall—we thought these were pretty neat little bikes—for the right person. Who is the right person? If you're thinking—"British bike=Norton Commando or Triumph TT or Vincent Black Shadow," then this is definitely not the bike for you. If you're thinking "Gee, I used to really love those British bikes. Tuning my Amal carb, adjusting my valves, putting out to the store on a Sunday morning to pick up the paper" then you might be the right person.

We would recommend this bike for a couple types of people— 1) British bike fanatics who'd be crazy to pass up this forgotten piece of history, 2) new riders who don't have the bread for a Harley, the stomach for a Japanese bike, and are handy and unpretentious, and 3) (maybe) ladies, looking for a light fun bike, as long as they understand the "tinkering" aspect.

OVERLEAF
LET FREEDOM ROAR
Photograph by Pulsating Paula

A special thanks to my friend, Pulsating Paula, an amazing woman who's been capturing the biker lifestyle through the lens of her camera for over 30 years. One of the most popular photographers to ever grace the pages of biker magazines, I am honored she allowed me to include this photograph.

We were gathering at Liberty State Park in New Jersey for a Rolling Thunder ride to the NYC Vietnam Veterans Memorial, the World Trade Center in the background, when Paula took this iconic photo. Circa 1990.

Keep your eye out for the upcoming biography of biker photographer "Pulsating Paula" Grimaldi-Reardon.

Daytona or Bust
It Only Took Thirty Years

Iron Biker News, November 1996

In '66 I heard about Daytona, a place where you could ride on
the beach and see some cycle races. There was no bike week, no
swap meet, no biker bars, no bikers (or at least we weren't
called that). There were races—plain and simple, races.

We talked about going that year. We even talked about riding—
I owned a '58 Beezer and Larry had a bike. In those days we
occasionally took a "long" ride, like Philadelphia to Atlantic City
(about 60 miles)—whenever we did it turned into a two or three
day adventure in the world of motorcycle repair. A ride from the
Northeast to Daytona, in the late '60s, for two eighteen year olds
would have been the trip of a lifetime (like the Fonda/Hopper L.A.
to New Orleans trip).

Well, we didn't make it down that year, or the next couple.
Larry went off to a life of long-haul trucking and I signed up for
marriage, kids, mortgage, 9-5, etc. Larry made it to Daytona a
couple times (in his rig, not his bike) over the decades, but even
though I kept riding, I never did make it.

Over the years what we originally wanted to see, races, became
secondary to what became the main event—Daytona became a
town that welcomed bikers (for a week a year), where you could
show up, not need to worry that motel owners would flip on the
"No Vacancy" sign when they heard your bike, and have a
relatively hassle-free week in a Florida seashore town with a bunch
of other bikers. Businesses that catered to bikers opened for
BikeWeek, and eventually some actually made Daytona their year-
round base.

Fast forward—30 YEARS! 1996, I still hadn't got to Daytona but suddenly I've got a lot a free time in my life—why not go to the now-legendary biker Valhalla, Daytona? Unlike 30 years ago, I've now got a pretty dependable bike, Daytona is running something called Biketoberfest (in October), so we decided to ride down. We had a nice ride, about 1,200 miles, mostly on the Interstate, never colder than about 45° and (till we hit Florida) never warmer than 75, and no rain.

We got to Daytona about five days before the event began, and checked into the Carol Inn; it's right on Atlantic Avenue and the front rooms open right onto the beach. Equally important, the folks who own the motel, Ken and Harsha, actively support BikeWeek and genuinely welcome bikers. These folks put on coffee in the morning, provide polishing rags, and generally do everything they can to ensure you have a good time. There were a couple other bikers at the motel when we checked in, and by the end of the week it was full of bikers.

What can I say about Daytona? It's a good place to vacation. There's a nice white sand beach—you can swim wherever you want and the lifeguards won't hassle you. If you want, you can get a day permit and drive your car or bike on the beach (at low tide).

There are lots of restaurants, and whatever you're looking for you'll be able to find. Every chain restaurant you can think of is there, so if you like Olive Garden, Denny's, Friday's, Beef and Ale, etc. it's there. If you're looking for more local flavor there's some really great places—Aunt Catfish's is a nice restaurant the specializes in local seafood dishes; it's all good and they give you plenty to eat. The Ponce Inlet Fish Camp preserves the fish camp atmosphere while you eat out on the dock or on a dry-docked cruiser. Good Mexican food at Rio Bravo by the airport. If you're looking for fancier there's Sapporo Japanese Steak House. All of Daytona expects casual dress, so jeans and T-shirt are fine everywhere.

Every merchant I met welcomed bikers—apparently Daytona is no longer an "in" place and if it wasn't for the bikers the local economy would collapse. There is evidence of the official support of bikers in the way Main Street was built—ramps at every corner so you can get your bike up on the sidewalk, and bike parking permitted on all the sidewalks of Main Street.

Of course there was also evidence of resistance to bikers. Daytona Shores, the town adjacent to Daytona Beach, went out of their way to stop and ticket any moving violation they could find—when they picked up my motel room neighbor and took him to County Jail they told him outright "We don't want no bikers in our town." Too bad—cause with an attitude like that pretty soon there won't be any. And where will they be then?

Main Street—ever been to a biker swap meet? Main Street is basically a big swap meet—there's vendors, some of them permanent and some there just for the week—more of them than you've ever seen before, and with more stuff. There's bike companies with Major Presence on Main Street. H-D of Daytona Clothing and Collectibles Store where you can pay a mere $375 for a leather-trimmed nylon jacket. Then there's the Easyriders store, where there's a humongous bouncer to make sure you enter the "In" door and where they sell all Easyriders products (and actually they are real nice in this store) and upstairs there's the "Bros Club" which is open to—you guessed it—Bros. And there's the biggest building on Main Street, the brand new, probably 10,000 square foot Mike Corbin Seats building—I'm not sure why you need something the size of an A&P to sell seats, but once upon a time I bought a Corbin seat. It came packaged in a box that said "Serious Parts for Serious Motorcyclists"—at the time I thought it should say "Expensive Parts for Stupid Motorcyclists"—after seeing his building now I'm sure.

Bars—here—there—everywhere. Bikers welcome everywhere.

Bikes—anything you can imagine (as long as your imagination is limited to Harleys, V8s and BMWs) is on Main Street. Stock, stretched, touring, V8, springers, girders, rigids, etc., etc.

People—well there's bikers everywhere, along with the cast of slightly off-center characters that you always find at biker events.

Races—don't know, never got to the speedway.

Rides—the weather is warm and nice, and there are beautiful scenic rides along the ocean and the river. If you're looking for different stuff to do, Disneyworld and the Kennedy Space Center are less than 90 minutes away.

I almost forgot—then there was H-D of Daytona. You almost have to see this place to believe it. Three years ago they built a new 20,000 square foot building, on about an acre of ground (an awful lot of land in a city). The building was designed to look like a hundred year old Spanish building, and it overlooks the Halifax River, so you can see it whenever you leave or enter Daytona (especially at night, when the whole thing is lit with neon). So we stopped in. As you know, none of the dealers have new Harleys for sale—guess again. This place has dozens of new bikes, which they claim are used???? Very interesting, since they have almost no miles on the odometer—but once a bike has been titled then Harley has no say about the price, so let's say you check out the dresser that in the Harley literature lists for $18,500—Surprise! Surprise! What you're looking at is a "used" bike, with 80 miles on the odometer, and it been "customized" with a new points cover, therefore it can be had for a mere $24,000. Then we went inside— over by the register was, very clearly posted, a "No Returns" policy—I don't know about you, but I don't buy things from people who won't stand behind them. Then we found a line of six or seven genuine custom bikes—the salesman told us they started at $35,000 and went to $70,000. None of these bikes, or the stock bikes, had price tags—a practice that makes me highly suspicious whether it's applied to home appliances or motorcycles. The long and the short of it—it was the most elaborate Harley shop I've ever seen, and the one place in Daytona that made me really uncomfortable.

Summary—want a nice vacation where bikers are welcome? Go to Daytona.

For several decades motorcyclists gathered informally at a little dairy bar in Connecticut; eventually the gatherings were formalized into scheduled Super Sundays, drawing tens of thousands. Torn down in 2011, the Marcus Dairy Bar is now just a memory, but oh what a fine memory it is. —Stu, 2014

Marcus Dairy
You Ain't Seen Nuthin' Yet

Iron Biker News, June, 1996

I'm an Old Fart—at least that's what my kids (and sometimes my wife) say—just because I think Al Bundy is a bigger star than Tom Cruise, or because I wear my belt 3 inches lower than I did 10 years ago? They also tell me I've got an "I've seen it all" attitude.

I don't really think I've seen it all, but I have seen an awful lot over the last 4 decades—an awful lot of bikes, bikers, old ladies, dealers, swapmeets, etc.

So as I travel around each year I go to a bunch of biker and motorcyclist events (completely at the expense of Iron Biker—ha ha), and I get to see an awful lot of the same stuff over and over. How excited can you get browsing (another) dealer table of black T-shirts, of biker jewelry, of leather—how stimulated are you by seeing another custom show, with the same six or seven classes, and often the same winning bikes—how much of a rise do you get out of yet another wet T-shirt contest (OK—so some things do get better all the time).

You get the picture. So Bob Steele calls one day and says we need to check out Marcus Dairy—my reaction was "waddafuck—are we givin' up Hogs for cows and chickens?" Well, once I understood that Marcus has a Swap Meet/Bike Show/Event Thing I got prepared to cover one more Biker Event (and I figured I could probably write the article before I even got there—cause after all, it was going to be one more event, just like all the others).

This is the thing—I wasn't at all prepared for what we found.

First of all, we get to this dairy in Danbury, Connecticut (which is much closer than any of us thought—it's just over by New York City), and—man! there was a *lot* of bikes. How many?—who knows? But I've been to a lotta lotta swap meets, and to Sturgis, and to every Rolling Thunder, and all I can say is—there was a *lot* of bikes. (The reported number was 30,000)

Then—uh-oh, they weren't all Harleys (but probably half were). So what do you usually see when you don't see Harley? Kawazuchi's and Yamasaki's right? Sheeeet—I started looking around and there were four-cylinder Indians, Indian Chiefs, Triumphs, BSAs, Nortons, BMWs, Ducatis, Cagivas, and there were some Yamahas, Hondas, etc., but some of them were serious crotchrockets, like a turbocharged V-Max (cause I guess 160 mph factory engine's not enough). Of course there were the even bigger American Bikes, the V8 Boss Hogs. (We entered the new Iron Biker custom, "Hardcore," in the Radical Class—these guys at Marcus clearly have good taste, giving us 3 trophies, the most for any bike in the class). All I can say is I've never seen such an assortment of street and exotic iron in one place at one time in my life.

Then of course there were the people. I'm always prepared for the usual cast of characters—the Regular Joe like you and me who get to a couple of these things a year, the young nubile (next Iron Biker covergirl) hardbellies, patchholders, born-again bikers, the heat, etc. What I wasn't prepared for was Doug Danger (wearing a Tux) who's out to break Evel Knievel's record, once he fully recovers from the coma he just came out of. Or ZAP, the blonde bombshell American Gladiator who makes regular appearances on TV's JAG—but here she was, flexing and signing autographs, right alongside the Ice Cream Man From Hell (we all know him, right), some Blue Knights, some Hell's Angels and some guys wearing multi-colored full racing leathers.

Then there was the swap meet—all the regulars were there: T-shirts, leathers, Harley parts, tattooists, etc. But then there were dealers selling stuff I've never seen at a swap meet before—the company auctioning off old BMWs, Kawasakis and Harleys—the guy selling portable $3,000 hot tubs—the table full of black metal weathervanes (for your roof) that look like Harleys—then, to top it all off, eight people who brought special seats for you to sit in while they give you a massage (no, not your front you pervert, your neck and your back) to relieve your tension (do bikers have tension?)

So I'll end where I started—you ain't seen nuthin' like Marcus Dairies. But if you go this year you're sure to see the Iron Biker crew again (and if you want to see your photo in IB you need one of three things—a fine bike, an interesting story, or a fabulous body).

For three months in 1998, the Guggenheim Museum exhibited 114 motorcycles. With the exception of some art and social critics who outright rejected this type of exhibit in an art museum, the show got positive reviews, even in the art world. And "The Art of the Motorcycle" remains the best-attended exhibit in the history of the Guggenheim. I hope you didn't miss it. —Stu, 2014

"The Art of the Motorcycle"
or, The Finest "Art Exhibit" I've Ever Seen

Iron Biker News, July 1998

New York City, the Guggenheim Museum. Ever heard of it?—Sure. Ever been to it?—Nah.

After all, when your choice for a sunny (or even gray) Saturday is riding or working on your scoot, or walking through the dimly lit musty halls of some museum to look at pieces of clay pots or 10,000 year old bones of animals that were dug up by bespectacled professors whose bones are a brittle as the ones they're digging, then the answer is pretty clear. Go for a ride—leave the museums to the school kids and senior citizens. After all, the bones, clay pots, sculptures and paintings aren't going anywhere—they'll still be around twenty years from now when you're ready to check it out.

Well, this summer (right now) there's a fantastic art exhibit in New York City. "The Art of the Motorcycle." Now, this is not paintings and sculptures of motorcycles—the exhibit *is* motorcycles. And these are not the motorcycles you'll see in your local custom or classic show, nor are these bikes you'll see at major events like Sturgis or Daytona. This is a collection of some of the rarest and most historically significant machines you'll ever see.

These bikes cover all eras, and represent a combination of the most unique and or/historically significant bikes of the day. For instance, could you cover the sixties and seventies without including the Easy Rider panhead or a representative group of Nortons, Triumphs and BSA's? But equally, could you cover that same era without including a Kawasaki triple, Yamaha 350 or Honda 50? Well, they're all in the exhibit.

From some of the coolest machines you've ever seen (Crockers, Harleys, V-8 land speed record machines, Vincents, Indians, and a lot more) to some of the most mundane, but significant machines of each era (Vespas, Hondas, Benellis, etc.). There's street bikes, racers, land speed record bikes—bikes that set production records and bikes that were strictly limited production. Some of the wackiest engineering ideas you could imagine.

The oldest bikes are from the 18'90s, and the newest from the early 19'90s.

Then there's the Guggenheim Museum, which is as unique as the show. The museum is round, and the entire center is open up to the roof. A ramp runs around the huge circular room; it starts at the top and goes down at a gentle angle winding you around (like a corkscrew) eventually down to ground level. I suppose you could start at the bottom and go up (working your way from the 18'90s bikes to present), or as we did, take the elevator to the top and work your way back through history (and walking down is so much easier).

This is not a huge museum—if this was a regular art show it would probably take an hour to walk down the ramp, stopping and looking along the way. Being that these motorcycles are very interesting, it took us about two hours to go through (there's more than a hundred motorcycles on display). Each bike has a placard explaining its' history and historical significance.

Also worth mentioning is the crowd. Mostly not motorcyclists — mostly tourists. But surprisingly these non-motorcycling tourists were finding the bikes (and it could also be the layout of the museum and the placards on each machine) very interesting. If you have a wife, girlfriend, etc. who is only mildly interested in bikes they may really enjoy this; my better half normally goes catatonic after looking at four or five hotrods or custom bikes, but she stayed interested through this entire exhibit.

There's also a great cafeteria in the basement level of the museum. Don't be thinking "high school cafeteria"; this is a gourmet food cafeteria. The food was great and, like the museum, different; I had a big bowl of cold carrot/ginger soup (they let me try it before I ordered) that was delicious. It is a little pricey, but definitely worth it.

If you love motorcycles, don't miss this exhibit; I've never seen such a diverse collection of machines in this condition anywhere before, and don't know if I will again.

04341077087-8

travel

When searching my archives for motorcycle articles, I came across my notes that are the basis of this next piece. I'm not sure why I didn't talk about this in my 2013 book, "Too Young for a Heart Attack"; I think I just plain forgot we did this. —Stu, 2014

World's Toughest Riders

Stu Segal, February 2014

In the mid-'90s I heard of an event called the Iron Butt Rally. The route was basically the perimeter of the USA—starting in Pennsylvania, going to Key West, then across to San Diego, up to Washington state, across the country to Maine, and back to Pennsylvania. In 11 days. 11,000 miles in 11 days!

Can you imagine that? On a motorcycle? Have you ever driven a thousand miles in one day? That would be roughly Philadelphia or New York, to Disneyworld; long drive, looonnng drive, the kind that requires several gas stops, and when you get out of the car at the destination everything aches and you just want to stretch, take a hot shower, and sleep for eight hours.

But no, imagine getting to the destination, washing off your face, laying down for say four hours, getting back in the car, and going right back. Oh yeah, and do this for eleven days straight. And make sure you average a thousand miles a day. This means you're definitely not getting seven or eight hours sleep a night, and you're not having a leisurely meal for 11 days.

Now think about doing it on a bike, without the comfort of heat or air conditioning. And did I mention, the way the route is laid out you will likely run into rain, sleet, snow, and temperatures in excess of a hundred degrees.

When I heard about this rally I was just fascinated that people were actually doing it. On bikes! I like to ride, and these are people who really like to ride. No girly-men here! Not even the women riders, who are clearly tougher than 99% of the male riders I've ever met.

The Iron Butt always stayed in the back of my mind, but like everyone, I was way too busy to consider such a ride. Especially considering the training I would want to do. At that time I was involved in starting up a business, a Harley dealership, that consumed every waking minute.

I learned that a rider actually had to qualify for the Iron Butt by documenting their endurance riding capability. The "easiest" qualifier is what the Iron Butt Association calls a "SaddleSore 1000"—very straightforward, 1,000 miles in 24 hours, documented.

Doesn't sound too hard, eh, a thousand miles in 24 hours? But have you ever actually done it? Back when we were kids, late teens/early 20s, we would drive straight through to Florida, only stopping for gas, hot dogs, pretzels, milkshakes. But oh yeah, there were generally two or three of us to split the driving. And it was always in a car.

But still, a thousand miles in 24 hours shouldn't be too hard. Going 70 miles per hour should only take 14 hours. *But* to average 70, would have to go a *lot* faster—after all, if, if, you could find a route that was all superhighway (which is pretty unlikely) you would still have to stop for gas ... and in those days I was riding a Harley, an Ultraglide, Harley's finest highway machine, and the safe range between fillups was 160 miles—so six gas stops. And, if it was going to take something in the range of 16-20 hours, I surely had to eat. And, um, could be some bathroom breaks might be needed vibrating around on a Harley for a whole day.

And really, the furthest I had ever ridden in a single day was 660 miles ... but the conditions that day were somewhat challenging. Tom and I were returning from Daytona Biketoberfest, and we got a late start, so we made it only as far as Florence, South Carolina, the first day.

Woke the next morning and it was a bit chilly, about 45 degrees, but we figured it would warm up as the day unfolded, so we had some coffee, some breakfast, and headed north on I-95, a long, straight, seriously boring road. It never warmed up as we moved north; went through Richmond with no problem, hit Washington DC late afternoon and luckily zipped around the Beltway. Just south of Baltimore Tom and I split, he heading northeast toward New Jersey, me heading due north toward Moscow high in the Pocono Mountains.

It was still in the low 40's, and now it started to drizzle. I had already gone 460 miles so I was thinking I would stop for the night, but then I saw a sign for York, PA . . . forty-some miles further, so I figured I'd get to York and have some dinner. I got to York, ate, warmed up some, and realized I was now only 160 miles from home!

Could I really stop in a motel only 160 miles from home? It was still drizzling, and the temperature was about 40, but I hopped back on the bike, got out on I-81, and headed north . . . most of the way drafting behind big-rigs so I wouldn't freeze. When I pulled into my garage it was 35 degrees, and I had come 660 miles, unplanned, in roughly twelve and a half hours. Freezing in the rain.

In 1999 I turned 50, and while age has never bothered me I am realistic enough to realize that as you age, your body becomes incapable of doing certain things. I was still fascinated by the idea of doing the Iron Butt, but endurance and strength decline as the body ages, and I was starting to realize that as tough as the Iron Butt is, it can only get tougher as one gets older. In my case, I had two health issues to deal with. First, at age 50 I was a 13 year heart attack survivor, but I took a cocktail of daily meds, and wasn't supposed expose myself to heat, cold, fatigue, stress, etc. And second, when I was in my twenties I had two herniated discs removed from my lower back; I always wear a back brace for support when I ride, but I had never ridden that far and just didn't know how my back would hold up.

And even the qualifier, a thousand miles in one day, was no stroll in the park. I figured "now or never", and resolved that while I was still in my fiftieth year I would do the qualifier, and keep the door open for a future run at the Iron Butt. In the back of my mind I knew I could do it; after all, I had done nearly 700 miles in the cold with a drizzling rain, and without really proper planning or preparation.

I started to figure out how to do this—a route that would be as free of traffic as possible, and as high speed as possible. Ways to eat and stay hydrated hour after hour. Comfort—it was going to be a long haul in the saddle. And training—just how to train for something like this?

Living just outside New York City it's a little tough to find roads that aren't clogged with traffic, some of them always, all of them sometimes; and I've come to learn over the years that when traffic will stop, at least here, is unpredictable. So the route needed to go away from the city, on a road and at a time that would be free and clear . . . and then continue on a route that would not hit major population centers. Also tough . . . leaving this area and going in nearly any direction proved challenging . . . Philadelphia, Hartford, Boston, Scranton, Harrisburg, Washington, Pittsburgh, Albany, all places to avoid.

I started looking at Interstate 81, which runs north/south, through the rural part of central Pennsylvania, and down through the Shenandoah Valley of Virginia . . . going through no major cities along the way. I could pick it up just outside Harrisburg, PA easily by taking Interstate 78 due west out of Jersey. So about 150ish miles, one tank of gas, to Harrisburg, then another 360 miles or so to Wytheville, just on the North Carolina/Virginia border . . . basically a NYC to North Carolina run. Make a U-turn, and ride back the same route . . . round trip, a little over a thousand miles.

Once I identified the route I became psychologically committed to the ride . . . and I started thinking, company. The ride would be more fun if I had company. Now I had been riding roughly 35 years, co-owned a Harley dealership, and knew *lots* of riders;

trouble was, 99.99% of them were either unwilling, or incapable, of doing a ride like this . . . the last thing I wanted was someone who couldn't ride, or whose bike was likely to break, or worst of all, would be whining about pain, fatigue, and anything else that might happen.

I had one friend who was *always* up for a ride. Never even had to tell him where we were going. If I said, "Do you want to ride to . . . ", the answer was always yes. Didn't matter if we were going for a half hour ride to the shore, or across the country. And he could ride. And he never complained. Like me, he was actually happier when riding, and the longer the ride the happier he was. So I called Tom McTamney, and before I finished the sentence he said yes. We decided to shoot for sometime in late September/October, figuring it shouldn't be too hot or too cold then, and a Saturday, to avoid both commuters and Sunday drivers . . . and we'd pick the exact Saturday based on the weather.

And then we came up with a brilliant idea—not only would we do a SaddleSore 1000, we would be the first ever to do it on Harley-Davidson Screamin' Eagle motorcycles. Harley had just released the first ever Screamin' Eagle bikes, the FLTRSEI Screamin' Eagle Road Glide[2] . . . these were fitted with high-performance engines, custom paint, and lots of accessories and chrome. They were fast, and cool. And coincidentally, Tom had a black/orange/white one, and I had a triple red one. What a great opportunity to not only qualify for the Iron Butt, but to exhibit the dependability of Harley's highest performance engine in real life conditions beyond what most riders would ever experience!

So now that I had company, back to my preparations. Staying hydrated wasn't going to be a problem; just like on the second trip to the Grand Canyon I would mount bicycle style water bottles on top of my saddlebags. And for nutrition, granola bars in a pouch

---

[2] For you Harley history nuts—the 2000 FLTRSEI was the first bike to ever carry the Screamin' Eagle designation. It was not the first CVO bike; the 1999 FXRS2, a project of the H-D parts division, was the first CVO bike, but it was not a Screamin' Eagle. Unlike the Screamin' Eagles, the FXRS2 and FXRS3 used stock engines.

on my dash. This should reduce the amount of time I needed to be off the bike.

Training? Two parts—physical and riding. I did daily exercises to loosen and strengthen my back, treadmill for cardio, and stuck to a strict diet to improve my general condition (and this went on for about three months). And I needed to ride (bonus!), only with a specific discipline. I needed to go a full tank of gas, 160 miles, without stopping or putting my feet down; the next week I rode two full tanks, with only a ten minute fuel stop in between. Then . . . well, you get the picture. And drink and eat while riding. I also did this for three months, knocking out a 600 mile day once a week the last month.

There was nothing to do but wait for a good Saturday, my hope being a clear, dry, 60-70 degree day. As we moved through September and early October, the Saturdays were all rainy, or stormy, or sweltering. Then on Thursday October 12th I saw what looked like a perfect Saturday forecast—at the north end of the route it was going to be about 50 degrees in the morning, and 500 miles south, in Wytheville, the high in mid-afternoon was going to be 74. No rain. Light wind. A more perfect day we couldn't hope for. And just in time, another week or two and the hawk would be upon us.

Friday I made sure everything was set. Water bottles full. Granola bars stocked. Tire pressures, oil level, airshocks all okay. Roadcrafter suit ready to go. And oh yeah, a full tank of gas— nothing worse than showing up for a ride, any ride, and waiting for the idiots who forgot gas. Tom and I had an unwritten rule— we always showed up fueled and ready to ride, nothing to do but throw a leg over the bike and blast off.

6:30AM, October 14, 2000, 52°, Tom and I met in the parking lot of Cross Country Powersports in Metuchen. We swung by the ATM on Main Street, each did a balance inquiry with our ATM card, and each got a receipt for proof that we were in Metuchen at 6:30AM. And then we rode.

Before we got a half mile, before we even left Metuchen, a big buck, frightened by the rumble of the Harleys in the peaceful predawn hours, darted into my headlight ... and thankfully kept moving. Missed me by inches. I was hoping this wasn't an omen, a half mile into a thousand mile ride.

We blasted onto Interstate 287, then onto I-78 West, the rising sun at our backs. The Harleys were purring at 72 miles per hour, we were passing traffic, and we were gobbling up miles before the inevitable morning rush of loony north Jersey drivers hit the roads. Sixty minutes later, hello Pennsylvania! Another ninety minutes, 9AM, the odometer reading 164 miles, we were in the center of the state, just past Harrisburg, pulling into our first fuel stop in Carlisle, PA.

We got off the bikes, fueled, I stretched my back while Tom got a SlimJim from the little convenience store. We were back on our bikes in less than ten minutes! Now we were on Interstate 81, rolling south through rural Pennsylvania, the big Screamin' Eagle bikes eating the miles easily. Through Hagerstown, Maryland and into Virginia. Past the exit for Winchester, the traditional starting point for rides on the Skyline Drive. Cruising past the beautiful Shenandoah Valley and Woodstock (Virginia), where 35 years before I was a cadet at Massanutten Military Academy. At 11:40 we pulled into Harrisonburg, Virginia, 330 miles on the odometer—we took a half-hour break, fueling, using the restroom, and eating.

Back on the bikes a little after noon, and we blasted down I-81; pulled into Wytheville, just short of the North Carolina border, at around 2:45, with 504 miles on the odometer. It was beautiful, sunny and 74 degrees. We fueled, rode over to the First Virginia Bank, again got ATM receipts to prove our whereabouts, hopped back on the bikes, and started the return trip home.

My recollection was that this was the only tough part of the ride, at least for me. We had been on the bikes about eight and a half hours, I had the little soreness you would expect riding a bike or driving a car that long ... but that wasn't really bothering me, it was expected, and I was used to it from other trips. What was getting me was boredom, hour after hour, mile after mile, with nary a break. And you know what boredom does when you're driving or riding—makes your attention wander, or worse, puts you to sleep.

I was drifting, mentally, my mind wandering . . . my Harley saved me. Now one of the things that Harley does best, indisputably, is sound systems. And the Screamin' Eagle Road Glide had the latest state-of-the-art system. The last thing I wanted was music . . . lull me to sleep even quicker. So I switched on the FM, and started a channel scan, eventually coming across a strong NPR station broadcasting "Car Talk", a show I had never heard before. Listeners called in, and posed their automotive questions to the hosts. "Why does my car idle rough?" "Why is my left rear tire wearing out before the others?" "How do I get into my car when it's frozen shut?"

The show saved me. It got my attention and woke me up. I listened to it all the way back to Harrisonburg, VA, which we hit at nearly 6PM, with 675 miles under our belts. And from Harrisonburg I knew we had one more fuel stop near Harrisburg, PA, then the final leg home. Four tanks of gas gone, only two left. Realizing we had 12 more hours in which to finish the remaining 325 miles, we took a half hour break to fuel and eat.

At about 8:30 we pulled in to Carlisle, PA again. Now we were getting a little tired, 14 hours on the bikes, so we again took a half hour break. Another 155 miles to go. It was of course dark by now, and cooling off . . . not uncomfortably, but the mid 50's of the evening were nothing like the mid 70's of the afternoon.

The final leg home. I looked in my mirror; Tom was where he was supposed to be, as always. Tom is one of the guys who gets it, who understands that when you're riding with someone, you are supposed to be in the right place, always, and doing the right thing, always. The right place? If you're following the right place is in the rearview mirror of the rider in front of you, always; you are not to be lagging, passing, or drifting. The right thing? Being predictable, always; not doing anything unexpected or being anywhere unexpected, ever. Truth is, your lives may depend on it; and Tom was rock solid, always; in all the thousands of miles we traveled together, I never saw him do one boneheaded thing. Which may be why he's had such a long, successful riding history.

Well, I'll admit it, we didn't blast through that last leg like we did the first five; rather than pulling out of Carlisle and rocketing back to Metuchen non-stop never taking our feet off the pegs, we threw in an extra stop. Just as we came over the New Jersey border at 11PM, with an hour to go, we pulled into a truck stop. Didn't need gas, didn't need food, didn't need bathroom; just needed to get off the bikes and stretch a bit.

We pulled in to Metuchen at 11:54PM, 17 hours 24 minutes, 6 tanks of gas, 1,011 miles after departing. The Screamin' Eagle Harleys, amazing; powerful, dependable, comfortable . . . and since we chose to do this after bug season, the bikes weren't even dirty. I wasn't tired, I wasn't hungry . . . my butt *was* sore, but I felt fine. And at nine the next morning, I was back on my bike.

Will I ever do the Iron Butt? 11,000 miles in 11 days? Will Tom? I dunno, but at least the door's open if we decide we want to go for it. In the meanwhile I'll proudly display my Iron Butt Association license plate frame, which unabashedly states, "World's Toughest Riders."

So You're Thinking of Going Cross Country, Eh?

Iron Biker News, September 1995

I've been riding a lonnnnng time—so long that when I began there was no such thing as motorcycle inspection or helmet laws, that people went to Daytona to see the races, and motorcycles were prohibited on the Garden State Parkway.

I've probably logged 150-200,000 miles on my bikes, but I've never been on a bike trip of more than five days. I'm sure you know all the reasons—don't have the bread, can't get away, bike not dependable, wife will divorce you, can only tie so much stuff on the bike, do it next year, etc., etc.

I've also got some good friends, who will remain nameless, (but if you happen to live in NJ, PA or MD and you know the owners of a custom cycle shop in Landisville, NJ, then you know who I'm talking about) who go cross country every year. They manage to do this regardless that they could easily come up with a similar list of why they can't go. In the 12 years I've known them they've never done less than Sturgis, and they've done as much as coast-to-coast with their daughter (in a sidecar) when she was ten.

So over the years I've heard a lot of stories about these trips, and how they're done. Although I've never had the right set of circumstances to do an extended bike trip, I've always listened in rapt attention and hoped someday I'd get the chance. Well, this year I knew I could get the time off, had decided it was time to update my trusty '86 Lowrider, so I got an FL type bike with the intention of going somewhere for 2-3 weeks.

Then I started thinking about all my friends had told me over the years, which amounted to:

- We're gonna get up every day at 7 o'clock.
- We'll be on our bikes at 8.
- We'll ride 150 miles before breakfast.
- Then we'll stop every 150 miles for gas.
- After we've gone 500 miles we'll start to look for a place to pitch our tents.
- Then we'll get up in the morning and do it again.
- Of course if it rains the plan is unchanged cause we've gotta do 500 miles a day.
- By the way, you should be prepared for your bike to break down in Bumfuck, which will be at least 50 miles from the nearest Harley dealer, who will sell you overpriced "Genuine" replacement parts, and will be glad to schedule you for repair a week from Tuesday; don't even try to explain that your bike is broken down in East Bumfuck and your old lady is sitting on the bike with a .45 keeping the locals from removing your luggage.
- Of course, don't worry too much about the old lady, cause most first timers stop talking after about day three, and if she makes it all the way there's a good chance that when you get home she'll kick you, kick your bike, and tell you that she never wants to see you or your friggin bike again.

So with this inviting picture in mind, I decided that a short ride (Atlantic Ocean to Grand Canyon) with my spouse and friends would be the ticket for this summer. So off we go, and—

"We're gonna get up every day at 7 o'clock."—OK, so I got up at 7 every day, and watched as everyone else wandered out of their rooms at 8, 9, ...

"We'll be on our bikes at 8."—In 2 1/2 weeks it happened twice.

"We'll ride 150 miles before breakfast."—Do the donuts and muffins and coffee and toast in the motel lobby really count?

"Then we'll stop every 150 miles for gas."—or maybe every 100 (or 75, or 50)?

"After we've gone 500 miles . . . ."—I haven't figured this one out; we actually went 5,000 miles in 11 riding days, so we must have been doing about 500 daily, but it always seemed that as soon as we pulled out we were looking for a motel to bed down again.

"Pitch our tents???"—Well they didn't get me on this one, but check with the poor also nameless biker (ex-Pleasantville, NJ cop) who actually bought a tent last year, and was practicing setting it up in the dark till the day before the trip, when he learned that the camping never gets any more rugged than a Motel 6.

"Then we'll get up in the morning and do it again."—True.

"Of course if it rains . . . ."—We took every conceivable piece of rain gear, totes, booties, chaps, waterproof boots, faceshields—we got lucky and probably didn't spend six hours in the rain.

"By the way, you should be prepared for your bike to break down . . . ."—I guess I'm really lucky, cause my local H-D dealer (Electric City H-D, Scranton, PA) did one hell of a job preparing my bike for the trek, and it never burped in 5,000 miles (so I never got the chance to see whether the Rapid City, SD dealer really does have armed guards to keep you in line during Sturgis bike week).

"Of course, don't worry too much about the old lady. . . . tell you that she never wants to see you or your friggin bike again."—OK so I'm really, really, lucky, cause not only didn't she complain, but halfway through the trip she started wondering how we could do an even longer one next year.

So here we are, 5,000 miles later, no longer cross-country novices. We know where Wall Drug is, and how to get to the Soo, aye?

If you've been thinking about doing a major trip, I'd give you four pieces of advice.

1. Be prepared.
2. Don't think of it as a 20-day trip, think of it as four 5-day trips in a row (great advice from my friends).
3. Don't worry about the rest of it—a bad day on the road still beats a good day at work.
4. Do it now, don't wait—nobody's ever going to be able to really describe what you're missing if you don't.

We found ourselves sometimes visiting cool, out of the way places, and started sharing them with other riders.

—Stu, 2014

Off The Beaten Path

Iron Biker News, February 1997

I usually have a specific destination in mind when I go for a ride. I might be going for a 15 mile ride, or a 1,500 mile ride, but I'm usually going somewhere. We often get so focused on the destination, that we forget everything along the way except that slab of asphalt right in front of our bike.

But did you ever take that little side road, the one with the sign that says "Covered Bridge, or "St. Tikhon's Monastery," or "Scenic Ride"? Too often we're in too much of a hurry to take those little diversions, or to seek out the interesting side trips along the way to wherever we're going.

A few years ago I started resenting trips that feel like Poker Runs—you get on your bike and ride and ride, and stop to eat and sleep, and ride and ride, and you get to your destination (like a Poker Run). Then you hang out, have a good time (like a Poker Run), then you get on your bike and ride and ride and sleep and eat till you get home. I started thinking, "Gee, if we've got to go 3,000 miles to get to our destination, isn't there a pretty good chance that there's something interesting somewhere along the way?"

Well, we started actively seeking those interesting things. The only (unwritten) rules we had are 1) they shouldn't be too far out of the way (50 miles maybe—but we have been known to alter our route to get closer to some of these places), and 2) we usually try to keep these diversions to under a half-day so we can still make some progress on our trips.

The kind of places we're going to cover in the next couple months are (and please don't be surprised if you haven't heard of these, they *are* off the beaten path) Warthers in Ohio, Conner Prairie in Indiana, the Lackawanna Coal Mine in Scranton, Fallingwater outside of Pittsburgh and Blue Cloud Abbey in South Dakota.

Now don't get me wrong—we did not take a trip to Indiana to visit Conner Prairie—but knowing it existed we "tweaked" our route to Sturgis enough to spend a pleasant half-day on our way.

The kind of places we are not going to cover are places like the Smithsonian Institution, Wall Drug, the Daytona Speedway, the Grand Canyon, etc. It's not that these places aren't worthy of coverage—it's just that they're so well-known and well publicized that first of all, you know about them, and second, if you want to know more it's easy to find out. So we're going to stick to lesser known, but still interesting, places.

This is the first month for what we think will be a regular monthly column that will cover some of the interesting things that we've found "Off the Beaten Path." Next month we'll cover the Lackawanna Coal Mine in Scranton. If you know of any interesting places that are Off the Beaten Path, and would like to write about them, please send your articles to me at Iron Biker News.

Off The Beaten Path
Conner Prairie, Indiana

Iron Biker News, February 1997

Our first stop Off the Beaten Path is Conner Prairie, in Indiana. How did we find this place? What were we doing in Indiana?

We were headed for Arizona (the Grand Canyon), but we picked the middle of a brutal heat wave to leave the east, and the day we left it was over 120 degrees in Arizona. So we decided to ride due west, through Philadelphia, Pittsburgh, and we were going to keep heading due west till the heat wave broke, then we would turn south and motor toward the Grand Canyon. It seemed a reasonable plan—rather than ride through the south, we would ride across (temperature) cool middle America. What we didn't anticipate was, by the time we reached Illinois the temperature in "cool middle America" was 106 degrees, and it was even hotter in Arizona. We ultimately turned north to get out of the heat wave, and wound up in Sturgis (I've learned since that when you go on a 5+ day trip with Bob Steel, all roads lead to either Sturgis or Daytona).

Anyway—on the way through Indiana we were running on I-70 (or some local roads that run parallel). We took about a 20 mile side trip to Noblesville, just north of Indianapolis. An interesting note—we stayed a night just outside Indianapolis, watched the Indy news, saw extensive coverage of race riots that were going on in the city, and when we got home were really surprised to hear that nobody had heard anything at all about the riots—I guess if it doesn't happen on the east or west coast it either isn't newsworthy, or it's easy to suppress coverage.

So we visited a place called Conner Prairie Pioneer Settlement. I suppose most of you have visited, or know of, Williamsburg, Virginia—the painfully accurate colonial era town. Conner Prairie is basically the mid-west version of Williamsburg—with some dramatic differences.

Williamsburg accurately depicts an east coast town on (for that era) the leading edge. Williamsburg includes many homes and shops which are historically accurate (gunsmith, bookbinder, silversmith, wheelwright, wainwright, blacksmith, etc.) Williamsburg actually depicts a pretty sophisticated town of the era.

Conner Prairie is a prairie town of the 1830's—there weren't many a gunsmith, silversmith, or bookbinder in a midwest prairie town. This is an accurate village of about a dozen buildings (some original) including William Conner's mansion, the Doctor's house, the weaver's house, the carpenter, blacksmith, potter and shopkeeper.

Like Williamsburg the town is staffed with occupants in period attire, who stay faithfully in character. One of us mentioned that she was from India, and had flown to the US—this brought hoots and howls from the cook who knew she was crazed . . . after all, only birds can fly.

These folks also practice the skills of the 1830's. You can watch the blacksmith forge axes, have a conversation about medicine with a very well informed 1830's "Doctor," or watch lunch being prepared over the open fire.

The day we visited, it was just a little more than a hundred degrees. True to the period, all the occupants were in full dress (it would have been morally shameful to uncover their bodies in the 1830's).

We thoroughly enjoyed Conner Prairie. I can tell you it certainly makes a person appreciate living in the 20th century.

There were a good number of visitors when we were there. I checked license plates in the parking lot—almost all were relatively local, further confirming the "off the beaten pathedness" of the place. This is one of those places that's as much a national treasure as Williamsburg, but simply isn't part of our national consciousness. We'd recommend it for an interesting half-day if you're ever passing through Indiana on the way to wherever.

Off The Beaten Path
Scranton, PA

Iron Biker News, February 1997

O K, so Scranton isn't exactly off the beaten path. Damn near everybody has passed through Scranton on the way to Niagara Falls, the Finger Lakes, skiing, or going somewhere—Scranton is the juncture of many major highways in the Northeast. As a result a lot of folks from all over pass through—but did you ever stop there?

Nah—why stop? Everybody knows that Scranton is just an old coal mining town, and is probably filled with people who have black soot on their skin and do a lot of coughing from Black Lung disease. Well, Scranton does have a coal mining heritage, but it might be a little more interesting than you think. There's a couple things definitely worth seeing in the Scranton area:

> *Coal mining.* Scranton wasn't *a* coal mining town—it was *the* coal mining town. When coal was king homes across the country burnt anthracite coal (much harder and cleaner burning than bituminous)—over 95% of the anthracite coal in the U.S. is under Scranton, and it was nearly the sole supply for the entire country. The coal industry collapsed 40 years ago, as cheaper cleaner fuels became widely available, and with it the economy of Scranton collapsed. Now, 40 years later, the Lackawanna Coal Mine is open for public tours. They take you down into the mine the same way they used to bring out the coal—in a little tiny railroad car which is lowered by a huge winch into the bowels of the earth. The guides are mostly children of the miners, and are very knowledgeable. They'll help you get a real appreciation for what it was like for the men, boys and mules

who spent their entire lives in the mines, only to reap that final reward of Black Lung which took so many of them. I was pretty skeptical going in, but found this glimpse into the past to be truly fascinating. The Mine is open for tours April-November, phone 717-963-6463

Steam Locomotives. The U.S. Park Service dedicated its newest National Park in July, 1995—believe it or not, that park is in Scranton and houses the largest collection of steam locomotion in the country. "Steamtown USA" was originally a privately owned attraction in New England which was purchased and brought to Scranton. Somehow (through pork barrel politics) the US Government was convinced to turn it into a national park, and they've spent millions on it. Steamtown has been expanded, a museum built, a fully operational roundhouse constructed and the whole thing is now run by Park Rangers and volunteers. Through most of the year (excluding winter) there is an excursion steam train which makes a 24 mile round trip to nearby Moscow—some beautiful scenery along the way, even though there really is nothing in Moscow (they say this excursion is spectacular during fall foliage season). For me though the main attraction was the Southern Pacific Big Boy Locomotive, the largest locomotive ever built. You've probably seen these in old movies—they were the huge engines that hauled freight trains of 100 cars or more through the mountains. The size of one of these is hard to explain—you need to stand between the drive wheels (which are much taller than my 6'1" height) or climb up the coal tender (over 14 feet high) to appreciate the enormity of this monster. The Big Boy they have was the last running one of its' kind—it was moved to Steamtown about 10 years ago under its own power. Steamtown USA is open year round 7 days a week, 9-5 (but excursion trains don't run in the winter), phone 717-340-5200

Scranton Furnaces. Iron furnaces, owned originally by the Scranton family for whom the town is named. These were the original industry, not coal—restored and open to the public.

US Route 6. Going west out of Scranton Route 6 is surely the most scenic road in Pennsylvania, maybe the East—but that's a different article.

Next time you've got a reason to go through Scranton stop and take in the sights. Make sure you also stop at Cooper's Seafood Restaurant, a very interesting place that has (I think) 176 kinds of beer on the menu; also try their Jalapeño Poppers (noted on the menu as Bill Clinton's favorite at Coopers). Phone 717-346-6883. This time getting Off the Beaten Path means getting off that Interstate—try it at Scranton, you may be surprised.

I am still as mad about this as I was when I wrote it, and still as disgusted that so few of us value our country and our freedom. —Stu, 2014

I Need Your Vote!

Iron Biker News, December 1996

I am mad as hell—you know, I'm always mad as hell about something. Billy Joel once sang a song about people like me—"Angry Young Man," but I've stayed mad so long that now I'm an angry old man. I read recently that grumpy crotchety guys have a higher incidence of heart attack—even with empirical data that says being angry is bad for me, I still get mad. I don't know about you—me, I just can't help it.

I once upon a time thought that as I got older I would leave the anger behind—my parents told me this and I believed it. Unfortunately it's not true. I remember first being really angry at society when I was about 13, when "they" killed our President. I didn't know who "they" were, so I was just hurt and angry in general. Then "they" killed our President's brother. Then "they" sent American boys off to fight in a God-forsaken country in Asia. Then "they" . . . . well, I could go on and on.

We live in a great country. We are maybe living in the best place at the best time in the history of the world. So why am I pissed off all the time at something or other? I guess it's because whether we want to or not we're compelled to accept some really stupid shit that we, and others in our society, do.

This month—what else could it be—the Presidential election. Now, don't get me wrong, I don't watch C-Span, I don't watch Face the Nation, and I don't make a hobby of politics. I treat politics a lot like I treat baseball and football—I don't really have the time or inclination to follow either sport, but when it gets to World Series or Superbowl time I get interested, bring myself up to speed on the players, the teams, the coaches, and I become a fan for the Series or the Bowl. Same with politics.

So this time around I got interested in maybe May, and followed the candidates' progress and positions as best I could while living the rest of my life. Now (and I know this is judgmental) the election looked kind of like this to me:

The Incumbent—Our President, who according to all the best polls, is distrusted by over 60% of the people in this country, ran on a platform that seemed to change every day. The man will say whatever the public wants to hear to get votes. Is he a conservative? Is he a liberal? Who knows—he changes policies as often as I change underwear (which is, incidentally, daily). He certainly does look good, and he speaks well. He has a winning smile and he has charisma. But, after the Gennifer Flowers allegations, the Whitewater mess, and his general "Ha-ha I pulled one over on you" attitude, 60% of Americans don't trust the man.

The Challenger—(if you could call him that) Bob Dole, the king of Boring. Where did they get this guy? I remember when he ran for Vice President a couple decades ago, and he sliced and diced his opponent in the debate—he was real sharp, and real mean about it. I always got the feeling that the nastiness, meanness and grumpiness were still there, being held in check, till he got elected. OK, so everybody knows that the Party ran him cause they "owed" it to him, but hey, give us a break, give us a candidate we can vote for.

The "Other" Challenger—Ross Perot. The Republicans and Democrats did everything they could to squash this guy, and they succeeded. Keeping him out of the Presidential Debate never let him have a chance to face Fiddle Dee and Fiddle Dum—they knew damn well if he got on a stage with them he'd embarrass the hell out of them, and he'd get more votes than he did last time around. So they froze him out.

OK—so what am I mad about. The President for being a shifty-eyed liar (the only difference between him and Tricky Dick is, Nixon looked dishonest)?—no, how can I be mad at him for being what he is? The Republicans for being stupid enough to run Rip Van Winkle?—no, it's impossible to get mad at a political machine that by its' very nature is corrupt. Ross Perot for not getting in the race earlier?—c'mon, this guy has spent more of his own money than you or I will ever earn trying to get his message out.

Nope—I'm mad as hell at you, or at least half of you. Only half the people in this country voted. The other half were—well, I don't know where they were. They were obviously doing something else very important—more important than voting. And what happened? A man who over 60% of you don't trust was re-elected to represent us, to defend us, to ensure the future for our children. I can't imagine what anybody in this country could be doing that would be more important than electing our public officials.

Why am I mad as hell? I remember when as a kid I could ride my bicycle without a helmet, in my teens I could buy gas for 28 cents a gallon, I could ride my motorcycle without a helmet, I could make my own decision about whether or not I should have car insurance, I could go to work at a job (just me, not my wife) and cause the government didn't hammer me on taxes and cause the dollar was strong I could raise my family on one salary.

This country has gotten economically worse and worse over the course of my life (and I'm under 50). When I was a kid, my Mom was at home—she was there to send us off to school and to give us cookies and milk when we got home. Most of my friends Moms were home too. Look around you at young couples raising kids—do you know any who are doing it on one income, or are they all forced to have two salaries to make ends meet? This is the single most powerful example of how our standard of living has slipped in the last forty years—it now takes two salaries to buy the goods, products and services that our parents could buy with one salary in the '50s.

In addition there's been a steady erosion of the freedom of choice—helmets, insurance, seatbelts, etc., etc. What's going to happen in the next forty years, how are our kids and their kids going to make ends meet? Will they need a permit to do things you and I do freely today? I don't know the answers, but I know this— if we don't get out and vote (all of us), then the decisions that affect our children and our children's children will be left in the hands of politicians and special interest groups, and we'll all be sorry.

This is not one of those things that can be undone later—you have to vote to ensure that the freedoms, privileges and standard of living we have today are preserved for our children. Elections are always in May and November, and the Presidential election is always November. Next time around, give up one night (to watch the debate), and get up 15 minutes early to cast your vote. Your vote does make a difference; it can make all the difference.

I was just so disgusted when not the first, or the second, or even the third, but the fourth woman surfaced alleging sexual problems with our president. And to be clear, this was not about party or politics, it was about my feeling that the president should be an example of American ideals to the youth of this country; one shifty-eyed lying president in my lifetime was one too many. — *Stu 2014*

Slick Willie

Iron Biker News, April 1998

It's the middle of March, 53 degrees, and I just got back from a ride. I just read Harley is building a gazillion new bikes this year, prices are coming down, and there's a new fixed fairing bike (Road Glide) for guys like me. New Jersey is finally moving to 65 mph. Life is good—of course, when life is good, it's tough to find something that makes me mad as hell.

So this month I am going to depart from my normal motorcycle pulpit, and talk about something else—Willie. Yep, Slick Willie, who wants Kathleen Willey to grope his Free Willy.

Are you getting a little sick of hearing all this stuff? First it was Gennifer Flowers, then Paula Jones, then Monica Lewinsky, then Kathleen Willey. Somewhere in between was a former Miss Arkansas. Then there's the countless minions that he groped who have either decided to keep their mouths shut, or are waiting for the right book deal to make their story public. It's on the news every night. It's on Nightline every night. It's on Crossfire every night. It's on Politically Incorrect every night.

The only story I remember that carried on as long, or made me so aggravated, was the Iran hostage crisis. Maybe you remember—

the show now called Nightline was originally a nightly ABC News Special Report—day 7,496 of the hostage crisis. It went on so long that when the crisis ended, the show had developed an audience, so it stayed on the air.

Maybe you also remember, that by the end of that crisis American morale was low—one of its lowest points ever. How embarrassing—we were being led by President Howdy Doody, whose idea of retaliation against oppression was to boycott the Olympics. How quickly that changed when a new president was elected—suddenly the US was again taken seriously.

And therein lies my problem. What does the world think of the US now? All the news that comes from here to the rest of the world is, at best, about a president who can't manage his personal life as well as most average men on the planet—at worst a man who openly abuses his power for personal satisfaction. Can any of you still honestly say—"I am proud of my president"?

This presidential silliness has not only lost us the respect of the rest of the world, it has diverted us from things that are genuinely important. For instance, did you see that Iraq has classified Bill Clinton as a "war criminal"? (You probably didn't see it, as the Kathleen Willey coverage was much better for network ratings.)

Think about what it means to be a war criminal. In the 60s the Israelis kidnapped a man named Adolf Eichmann from South America. He was a hateful little man who ran one of the Nazi concentration/extermination camps were Poles, Jews and others were gassed by the tens of thousands. They took Eichmann back to Israel, where they hanged him. Was there an outcry from any country anywhere when they snatched Eichmann? Of course not, because he was a war criminal, a monster who deserved what he got.

Now our own president has been labeled a war criminal (and he's not even the president who ordered the Gulf War). This means our president could be kidnapped, dragged back to the Mideast, and hanged for war crimes. Let me tell you—it's not okay with me that anybody anywhere can label our president as a war criminal. (I personally would the find the act of labeling our president a war

criminal as an act of war against the United States.) My point is—
we are so diverted by the shenanigans of Willy's Willie that we are not
paying attention to the genuinely important events in the world, and
neither is our president or Congress. Willie, please do us all a
couple favors, 1) keep Little Willie in your pants for the rest of
your stay in the White House, 2) answer all the allegations
truthfully (if you know how) and put this matter to rest, 3) if you
can't do that, then resign and let someone who our children can
look up to live in the White House. (You could always do what
other guys your age do – cry "midlife crisis," tell your wife you
need some space, buy a Softtail Custom, get some tattoos and a
ponytail, find a 19-year-old who's never heard of pre-nups or
community property, and meet us in Sturgis in August.)

With the exception of the one who resigned, I have had
tremendous respect for all the presidents the last half of this
century, even though I've not always agreed with their politics.
They've all been fine individuals who have earned our, and the
worlds, respect. Willie, do the right thing – restore the respect we
expect and deserve from our president.

too young
for a
heart attack

too young
for a
heart attack

In 1987, when I was 37, I had a heart attack, a serious one. I had spent the day at the at Atco Raceway in New Jersey, at an event we looked forward to all year, the East Coast Hogfest. And, right up until the heart attack, it was a great day.

The folks at Atlantic County Harley always did a terrific job with this event. Drag races, ride-in bike show, swap meet, food, music, and then of course the other fun stuff—bike smash (yep, in those days folks were willing to pay a couple bucks to take a sledgehammer to a Honda), wet t-shirt contest, tattooists, and on and on. Hot beautiful weather. Couldn't ask for more.

Went home for what was planned to be a Fathers' Day dinner, but instead of sitting down to the celebratory meal with my wife and kids, my wife was rushing me to the Emergency Room. I'm lucky to be here ... at the very moment I was rushed in, on a Sunday night when most of the Docs are on their own time, an off-duty cardiologist happened to walk through the ER; he saved my life. Really.

But it left me damaged and limited in ways which challenged my ability to do a lot of the "normal" things that everyone does. One of those things is motorcycling—a little tough to do when your body can no longer tolerate heat, or cold.

In 2013 I wrote a book called "Too Young for a Heart Attack" to help young heart attack survivors cope. I talked about riding in spite of the heart condition, going cross country in the summer, in hundred degree weather, doing things that most heart attack survivors consider out-of-reach . . . not so, with the right attitude and proper precautions.

Here are two excerpts, our "trips to the Grand Canyon."

This first trip happened in 1991. It is excerpted from a chapter entitled "Cardiac Cripple," which suggests that certain patients become psychologically crippled by the knowledge of their disease, and by an obsession with every little ache and pain. The message of the chapter—don't allow your condition to become a self-fulfilling prophecy which prevents you from living your life.

—Stu, 2014

Excerpt from "Too Young for a Heart Attack"

Scaling the Grand Canyon

A few years after the heart attack, I was feeling some discomfort. Not serious, but real. I was breaking into sweats every time I exercised; but much earlier and easier than normal. And I had this strange uncomfortable feeling that radiated up into my throat. Only when exercising. A common symptom of blockage in an artery is pain when exercising, in the chest or back, or radiating into the arms or throat . . . which subsides when the heartbeat returns to normal. Which mine did. It wasn't horrible, but it was there.

Two possibilities . . . go to the doctor, or wait and see. Normally, I would have gone to the doctor, but my future wife, Rashmika, and I were planning a motorcycle trip in a few days and I knew the doctor would have me in the hospital for an angiogram if he heard these symptoms. I figured the symptoms weren't that bad, only occurred when exercising, so I would go on the trip . . . and take it easy . . . and call the doctor upon my return.

Off we went, to the Grand Canyon . . . of Pennsylvania. About a 5 hour ride, through the Delaware River Water Gap and across the beautiful Endless Mountains of northern Pennsylvania. We left in the morning, but meandered, stopping along the way for lunch, for ice cream (I had frozen yogurt), and to check into the hotel.

We arrived at the Grand Canyon at about 4 p.m. on a beautiful summer day. It's actually a gorge, a very large gorge, which stretches over 45 miles and has depths as great as 1,500 feet. It is very different from "the" Grand Canyon; the GC of PA is beautiful, lush and green, and is not nearly the size of "the" Grand Canyon. We were at the northern end of the gorge, looking down into the canyon, and noticed a sign, "Turkey Path," which indicated a trail leading to the floor of the canyon.

The sign also said "WARNING! As sections of this trail are narrow, steep and hazardous, proper footgear should be worn." We started down, wearing our motorcycle boots of course. It was a gentle decline, a "switchback" trail which descended up and back across the face of the mountain into the gorge. After walking for a long time we encountered folks coming up, and I inquired whether we were near the bottom—they laughed. A little further on we ran into the sign, which read "You are now halfway. Think about how far you have come before proceeding." Big deal, on we went.

Eventually, after descending over a mile of switchbacks, we reached the canyon floor, and that is what was there . . . the floor. Dirt, trees, leaves. I looked up, and could no longer see the sun overhead. "Hmm," I thought, "must be starting to set." Not a very attractive proposition, being at the bottom of this canyon after sundown. Did I mention there were no lights on the trail? No park rangers? No flashlight? No cellphone (early 90s)? We needed to get out of there, and we needed to do it before the sun set, or we would probably be stuck there until morning. I envisioned us huddled together, shivering.

We started up the trail immediately. The first five minutes was fine, then I realized that the gentle switchback trail wasn't really so gentle . . . going up. Matter of fact, it was already starting to feel steep. Now since then, I've done the math, and that switchback trail climbs at a 15 percent grade; next time you encounter a serious hill in your vehicle, the kind of hill that has warning signs indicating the grade for trucks, check it out. I think you'll find a 15 percent grade is serious.

As we're climbing I'm thinking about pacing myself, and keeping proper posture. But my breathing is becoming labored, and I'm starting to sweat. Rashmika, who is always cold, is behind me and is starting to complain that her leather jacket, which she is now carrying, is too heavy (yes, even though it's summer, and more than 70 degrees, she is wearing a heavyweight motorcycle leather jacket). So I grab her jacket, and throw it over my shoulder.

Driven by fear of being stuck after dark, we climbed that trail vigorously. Sweating, breathing hard, legs aching. A 15 percent grade that goes on for a mile is serious; much much more serious than anything I did in my daily life, and much more serious than anything ever thrown at me in a stress test. I was probably well beyond my target heart rate, and for a long time. We collapsed when we got to the top.

Before leaving for the trip, I had never mentioned to Rashmika the discomfort I was feeling. (Matter of fact, she never knew of it until she read this book.) But lying on the ground after that climb, I realized I was feeling none of the symptoms which concerned me. Felt fine the next morning and thereafter. The Grand Canyon challenged me with a much greater stress test that the doctor would have; my fears were quelled. Whatever the symptoms I felt, I knew they weren't coming from my heart.

In 1995 we decided to ride from the Atlantic Ocean to the Grand Canyon, in summer of course, something definitely not recommended for heart patients. I talked about this trip in my chapter called "Coping with Limitations," as an example of how something that seems totally out of reach can be accomplished with some determination and a little common sense. —Stu, 2014

Excerpt from "Too Young for a Heart Attack"

Riding to *the* Grand Canyon

Let me tell you about one of the "activities" that really challenged some of my limitations. In the mid-90s, Rashmika and I decided to go on a cross-country motorcycle trip with our friends, Tom and Lucille. The general plan was to head west. We would spend the first night in Pittsburgh, visiting our son, then continue toward the southwest, eventually reaching the Grand Canyon. We would then take a different route back across the United States. In August.

One of the initial things I did was visit my cardiologist. She was an extremely sharp, talented, caring doctor, and I valued her opinion. I told her the plan, and asked her advice—her reply, "Don't go." When I pushed harder for suggestions, she kept giving me the same answer, "Don't go." She stopped short of saying, "You'll die" (but I could tell that's what she was thinking). I was not deterred.

Next stop, general practitioner Dr. David George, a doctor with an old-fashioned approach to medicine. He was very pragmatic, and was just as willing to use tried-and-true home remedies as he was to prescribe modern medications. His response was very different. He advised me to make sure I stayed fully hydrated throughout the trip, and do my best to avoid excessive heat—

actually, he suggested riding in the early morning and at night. This made me feel better; at least he wasn't reacting as though it was going to be a one-way trip.

When I got home, I went to work on solving the hydration problem. I mounted bicycle water bottle cages on top of the saddlebags of my Harley-Davidson, so that while riding I could easily grab a water bottle. Hey, if it worked for Greg LeMond on his 2,000-mile Tour de France win, it should work for me. I just had to remember to do it.

The first night of the trip we arrived in Pittsburgh as planned; when I watched the weather report I saw the temperature in Arizona, near the Grand Canyon, was 112 degrees. So we modified our route a bit, and headed due west to New Philadelphia, Ohio, where we visited Warther's cutlery and museum, where they still today make some of the finest cutlery in the world, using the same methods and materials they did 100 years ago.

The next day we wound up at Conner's Prairie, sort of a Midwestern farm town version of Williamsburg, Virginia; the town was of course not air conditioned, and was sweltering. By the third night we were in Peoria, Illinois; the temperature reported at the Grand Canyon had risen to 117 degrees.

So we continued west, but moved slightly north. By the next afternoon we were in Ames, Iowa; believe it or not, by 1 p.m. it was 105 degrees in Ames. We headed for a local mall, where we sat in the air-conditioning and took in a movie.

Though we kept checking the weather reports every night, we never saw the temperature drop in Arizona, so we continued west and slightly north, eventually arriving in Sturgis, South Dakota. Sturgis is the home of the largest motorcycle rally in the world, but we were actually a week early (not a surprise, as we never really intended to be there at all). We had a great time in Sturgis, hanging out with all the vendors as they pulled in to set up. We also got to see the amazing sights of the Dakotas and Wyoming—Devils Tower, the Black Hills, the Crazy Horse Memorial, Mount Rushmore, the Badlands. At one point, we shared a small, narrow road with a buffalo that dwarfed us, towering over Rashmika, me, and our Harley.

And let me mention, the trip did not prevent doing the other things necessary for my health. I was able to still eat carefully everywhere we went. I exercised every day—I was up every morning early, and took my daily walk before breakfast. Actually, Lucy was recovering from a health issue, and also wanted to exercise to get back in shape. So many mornings I had company on my walk, and it was a great way to start the day.

Still trying to stay out of the heat, we decided to make our return trip in the north, so we crossed the most northern states and eventually got to the other side of the Great Lakes, entering Canada at Sault Ste. Marie. We rode east across Canada, took a ferry boat across Lake Huron, rode through Toronto, and eventually came back into the United States at Niagara Falls. Even though we never made it to the Grand Canyon (the one in the southwest), this was one of the most memorable trips ever. Four thousand miles outdoors filled with buffalo, prairie dogs, mountain sculpture, motorcycles, and the beauty and majesty of America.

Had I followed the advice of the cardiologist, a woman who I truly trusted, it would never have happened. Am I suggesting that you not follow the advice of your doctor—no! What I am suggesting is this—know your doctor, and know yourself. I have not known many cardiologists, but the ones I have all have something in common—they err on the side of caution. I suppose this is because the decisions they make can be life or death, and neither they, nor any reasonable person, is going to advise another person to take risks which could be deadly.

Somewhere between the cardiologists' cautious point of view of what is acceptable, and living a totally unrestrained uninhibited life, most likely lies the reality of what you can do. Had Rashmika and I completely ignored pragmatist Dr. George's advice, and followed our original plan to ride to the Grand Canyon, where the daily highs were exceeding 110 degrees, it may have indeed been a one-way trip for me. But taking some reasonable steps to ensure I didn't exceed limitations allowed me to have one of the great adventures of my life.

riding tips

Shut Up and Ride
(or, how to prepare for your summer trips)
Iron Biker News, December 1997

This time of year I sometimes wear a T-shirt that says "SHUT UP AND RIDE" in huge letters on the front. I wear it when I go on vacation. To me, a vacation is a time when I can get up in the morning, and spend the day riding.

I've found the best way to ruin a vacation is to have it turn from a riding vacation, into a "motorcycle repair" vacation. You know what I mean—here you are 2,000 miles from home, going down the road at 60 mph, and you hear a terrible noise, the bike lurches, bangs, shudders, and coasts to a stop. You look down the road, and what do you see—well, Lordy, there's your drive chain lying in the middle of the road. You run back, grab it, and believe it or not it's unhurt—somehow the masterlink fell out. No prob—you just grab your toolkit, dig down and find that spare masterlink . . .

No sweat right? Until you look in your saddlebag and realize that Junior borrowed your toolkit to fix his bicycle, so instead of being in your saddlebag it's scattered all over your neighborhood in the garages of all the seven year olds whose bikes have broken in the last year. So now—where do you find a masterlink on a Saturday at 7PM on a two-lane road in northern Louisiana 30 miles from a town? You know the answer—you're going to flag down somebody, try to get to town (while your bike sits on a road), try to find the right masterlink for your O-ring chain—and there's a good chance you're going to be down in a local motel for a day and a half.

The alternative? 1) Check out your bike before your trips, and 2) bring a proper (for you) toolkit.

Check out your bike. If you're going to travel, and enjoy it, your bike needs to be relatively trouble free. The only way to make that happen is to maintain the bike.

Do the manufacturer's recommended maintenance. If you decide the manufacturer's recommendations are not right, that's okay—as long as you decide to maintain the bike more often than recommended, or you decide on parts, fluids, etc. that exceed the manufacturer's recommendation. Don't cheap out here and decide to put reconditioned oil in your engine to save a dollar a quart, or to pour in that GM brake fluid cause you have a leftover can, or to wait 8,000 miles between oil changes cause that's what Ford recommends for your car—these types of decisions will cause you lots of grief. Read your owner's manual and follow, or exceed, the recommendations.

You need to check out your bike a week or so before your trip. In addition to doing the service, make sure you check stuff like tire wear, tire inflation, cables frayed, electrical connections tight and (dielectric) greased, chain or belt tension or wear, loose nuts and bolts, etc. Check everything you can, and if you don't feel you have the capability to do it comprehensively, get a qualified shop to do your service before trips.

Also—*fix stuff*. When you hear a little rattle, hum, rub, etc., *fix it*. Do not develop the "The bike still runs so I'll just ride and see if it's okay" approach. When you hear or feel something unusual, this is an indication of wear—if you decide to just wait you'll probably get used to the noise, but whatever it is will just break in time. When that little whirring noise you've been hearing for the last week or so becomes a blown transmission in the middle of your trip, it'll sure ruin your day.

Don't test new accessories on trips. A lot of improvements I've made to my bikes have been for long-distance touring. I now avoid the temptation to install some accessory the night before a trip—too often when you install something new it needs adjustment, and you need time to get acclimated to the new accessory as well. Leaving on a trip with something new really sets you up to be messing with it (or worse, suffering with it) your whole trip. Now, before I go on a 5,000 mile trip, I try to do a 1,000 mile trip just to make sure everything works OK.

TOOLS—This is actually a tough thing to recommend, because there are a couple factors that differ with each rider:

1. How much room you have on your bike for tools (and spare parts)?
2. What is your mechanical aptitude?
3. What can you reasonably expect to be able to repair at roadside?

Don't worry about how much room you have for tools—you have enough. On a dresser, use the saddlebags and the fairing lowers, on a cruiser use a leather toolbag. On a lot of bikes there's hidden unused space if you look for it—for instance, on the FXRs there's space under the seat, and if you buy a "stash tray" you can lay a small toolkit under the seat without shorting out your battery.

How about your mechanical aptitude? I can't answer that, but I do know that most Iron Biker readers are Harley riders, and most Harley riders are not afraid to do some tinkering. This doesn't mean we can all do a valve job on our bikes, but it does mean that most of us know how to fix a tire, install a battery, change spark plugs or a chain, adjust a clutch, etc. So when you're selecting tools for a kit, stick to stuff that you know how and when to use.

What kind of stuff can you reasonably expect to repair at roadside? Tires, chains, lights, fuses, adjustments, sparkplugs— and maybe more. Are you going to be able (or willing) to fix a pulled-out cylinder base stud, or a broken transmission mainshaft—no, and that means you can leave your ring compressor and micrometer at home. Bring tools that you need for roadside repairs.

What I keep in my toolkit is:

Set of sparkplugs
Wireties
Electrical Tape
Flat tire kit
Tire gauge
Swiss army knife
Rag
Adjustable wrench (large crescent—with about 4" of the handle cut off so it'll fit in my toolbag)
Adjustable wrench (box)
Small visegrips
Open end wrenches 3/8—9/16
Ratchet and socket wrenches (1/4" drive to save space)
Spark plug wrench
Screwdriver (straight/Phillips combo)
Complete set of Allen wrenches
Complete set of Torx wrenches
Owner manual (or photocopies of the pages you need)

This whole mess fits in a leather toolpouch that's 12"x6"x3," and weighs about 10-12 lbs. I consider this just the most basic tools, but staying within my capabilities to do roadside repairs it's enough for me to make a difference. (The truth is—no matter how much I put in my toolkit I never feel like it's enough—which makes me even more fanatical about preventative maintenance).

NOTE: Of course now we have the universal fix-it-all tool, the cellphone. Regardless, I still carry a toolkit. The cellphone can find you roadside assistance, which is great if you have a problem so serious you can't repair it yourself, of if there happens to be a nearby open repair shop willing to fix your problem right now. I'm not suggesting you leave your cellphone home; I am suggesting you be prepared to deal with some of the more common problems yourself to minimize your inconvenience. —Stu, 2014

Suggestions for how to ride in the cold weather and stay comfortable. In the last 20 years winter riding gear has improved immensely, newer high-tech materials, and great new vendors (including Harley-Davidson, who I hammered in the article for their archaic approach decades ago). And, of course, heated gear . . . the greatest! But the principles presented here remain sound, and when used with modern gear work even better. —Stu, 2014

Riding Season?

Iron Biker News, December 1996

E very year I hear folks from my area (New Jersey/Pennsylvania) refer to the "Riding Season."

Now since these folks live where I live, their riding season should be the same as mine, right? Wrong. Years ago I noticed in November bikes started to disappear from the roads, and by Christmas each year there were hardly any bikes on the road, and they typically didn't re-appear till early spring.

See, I hate the cold weather, so I didn't understand how come I was out on the road 11-12 months a year and no one else was. Certainly it wasn't the weather; except for certain days each year (when it was either snowing, raining, or the roads were icy) the weather was ride-able; in fact, all winter long you find those occasional cold, clear, dry Sundays that are so refreshing.

I started watching and listening to other bikers and found the answer (obvious) was clothing—now don't decide I must be some kind of "cold weather freak," I really do hate the cold so keep reading. I ride with everybody (but mostly with Harley people) and I started noticing some definite clothing trends that prevent riders from taking advantage of the full year round mid-Atlantic riding season.

Most folks I know wear boots, jeans, light leather and light gloves during the spring-summer-fall, and for the winter they adjust by going to a heavier leather, heavier gloves, chaps and a scarf. They extend their riding season by maybe 45 days twice a year (spring and fall) but still can't hack winter; the reason is obvious—leather, chaps and a scarf just won't make it. Sure, it looks cool—but is looking cool worth giving up riding your bike for 4 months a year?

Over the years, I've developed three distinct levels of riding clothes (not counting of course that you always need to be prepared to get rained on).

- Light—late spring, summer, early fall—you don't need me to tell you about this.

- Colder, down to about 45 degrees. This is what most folks wear for "cold"—chaps, leather, scarf, gloves, maybe thermals (and something I've found works real good—a pair of long johns cut off about Bermuda short length to wear under your jeans and keep warm that area your chaps leave open). Dressing like this still lets you look relatively stylish, keeps you kinda warm—but as you know just won't make it on a damp 22 degree day in February.

- Cold, 45 degrees and down. You know, once it gets below about 45, and you consider the speed of your bike, and the "wind chill factor" it's not at all unusual to be riding in wind chill factors well below zero, in fact sometimes the wind chill factors you encounter are similar to a winter day in Antarctica. Your approach to this level of cold must be very different if you intend to remain comfortable (and that's the key to year-round riding—comfort, not merely perseverance).

Your own body heat is absolutely enough to keep you warm in winter! The trick is how to keep your body heat from escaping.

There are generally two factors, but for motorcycling there are three, 1) layering, 2) wind breaking, and 3) sealing it all in:

1. *Layering*—several layers of heat retaining clothing to keep the heat close to your body but to allow your sweat to evaporate.

   Go to your local ski store, or maybe Army/Navy store. Start with long johns made of Thermax, Duofold, or the like (I like Duofold)—about $40. Then socks—I generally look for two-layer, polypropylene/wool—about $12. Then put on your jeans, a thermal shirt (yes, over the long johns), and a sweatshirt—remember, one of the advantages of layering is you can take stuff off if you get hot.

   Now there's two more items of underclothes you need—boot liners and glove liners. At the ski store you can find these space age metallic liners (shiny silver fabric) that skiers wear. These suckers actually generate heat, and a pair of boot and glove liners together will cost you about $18.

   That's it for underclothes.

2. *Wind breaking.* Now you need outer garments that will both break the wind and hold in the heat.

   Don't bother to screw around with leather, it's too heavy, not pliable and simply doesn't work in extreme cold. You need something that's light enough to move around in comfortably, even with all those layers of clothes, and warm enough to hold in all the heat, from your ankles to your neck.

   Save yourself a lot of work; get down to your local motorcycle or snowmobile shop and buy yourself a winter riding suit—something that is designed for a riding position, and for high wind speeds. These are typically two-piece suits, a coverall and a jacket and are usually made from incredibly effective materials, such as Goretex on the outside and Thinsulate insulation. There are many good manufacturers, just make sure to check that you're getting the high-tech stuff you need (Thinsulate, Goretex, Polartec, etc.)—do not buy some heavy duty piece of Genuine Motorclothes from you-know-who that has exotic stuff like "filled with 100% polyester)—if that's what you want go to Bradlees and buy a $28 jacket (it won't keep you warm, and neither will Harley's latest "Cold Weather Explorer Suit"). A decent suit will cost probably $200-300; of course I have been wearing the same one since 1987.

3. *Sealing it all in.* This is the really tough part—sealing in the heat, and keeping out the wind. I'll go over this from bottom to top, assuming you are now layered and are standing there in your cold suit.

First, put on your boots. Tuck your pants in your boots, and then put your cold suit over your boots.

Next, your neck and head. Before you put on your helmet, put on a headover (baklava)—this is kind of like a ski mask, with an open face—I recommend polypropylene; also a ski shop item—about $10. Cover your head, tuck into neck of cold suit, seal neck of cold suit, and put on helmet. This will not only keep your head and neck warm, it will also prevent wind from getting in your collar. (Note: I love the "wind in my face" but in the winter I put an anti-fog face shield, about $20—these are readily available at most Non-American motorcycle shops).

Finally, (not forgetting you're already wearing your glove liners) your gloves. This is the one place leather still seems to work for me. Heavy leather gauntlets with thinsulate lining do me OK down to the low 30s, below that I switch to leather gauntlet mittens lined with thinsulate, still over my glove liners.

Now, I know that all sounds like a lot of work, and a lot of money, but let me summarize for you:

- You spent $??? thousand dollars on your bike, and it gets parked for the winter.

- You see other nuts on their bikes in February, and you always figured they were freezing their butts off.

- If you spend a little cash, ($300-400) you too could be riding most months every year, and not freezing.

It sounds like a lot more hassle than it really is. Once you've got it down to a system, it'll take you less than ten minutes from the time you get your jeans on till the time you're completely ready to face the weather.

Spend a few dollars, give it a try. I know you'll get the same feeling of satisfaction I do when I roll out on a bright sunny February day for a "Sunday ride," and you'll get lots of pleasure out of laughing your ass off at the fools who invariably ask: *"Aren't you cold?"*

Water Soluble Motorcycles?

Iron Biker News, June 1999

I'm not usually really "Mad as Hell" when I write these articles, but this time I am.

My friend parks his motorcycle outside while he's at work. Should it start to rain he is invariably approached by a stream of people telling him it's raining (because they think he'll want to move his cycle inside). When he doesn't react by running out and pushing in the cycle, they almost always ask why. His reply, always, is "I don't own one of those water-soluble Harleys."

His response is a result of his long-term observation that some Harley owners act as though they, and their bikes, are water soluble. As though you actually can't let your Harley get wet, or ride it, in the rain. Now admittedly, riding in the rain increases certain risks, and requires a higher level of attention to certain details than does riding on dry roads. And also the increased level of attention required may be a little more stressful and cause fatigue quicker than riding on dry roads. But there is no reason not to ride in the rain, and clearly no reason to hide your motorcycle from raindrops.

For yourself, you need a decent rainsuit—a relatively inexpensive item you can purchase at any motorcycle dealer. I'd also advise either rubber booties (available at cycle shops), totes, or waterproof boots. Maybe gloves if you don't like wet hands (never really bothered me). And for sure either goggles or a faceshield so your vision doesn't become impaired by squinting.

For your bike—nothing. Your bike is not water soluble, and all you really need to do is dry it off once it stops raining. As long as you're keeping the bike properly maintained and waxed you won't have a problem. I am of course assuming that you have taken care of the safety needs of your machine—good tires, good brakes, proper rubber handgrips and footpegs (sure, billet footpegs and handgrips look good, but become way too slick when wet). For serious touring, you probably want to consider a windshield—at highway speeds a good windshield diverts most of the water around you.

Riding technique—you need to pay attention to details in the rain. Do not pull your front brake first in the rain—I use my front brake as little as possible when the road is wet. Pay attention to the road surface, as the combination of oil on the road, covered with rainwater can be as slick as ice (so stay out of the center of the lane where the oil drippings from cars accumulate). And remember, the road is equally slick for everyone, so be cognizant that other vehicles may react differently than on dry roads. Increase all your safety margins to compensate—give yourself more distance from other vehicles than you normally would.

Maybe you've never gone on a vacation on your motorcycle. If you have, you realize that eventually it's going to rain. Once it starts to rain you have two choices (if you're on vacation)—one choice is to stay in and "outwait" the rain, and this is not always a great prospect—after all, who wants to spend their vacation locked in a motel room, tent, etc. The other choice is to learn to deal with the "less than ideal conditions," like rain, and still enjoy riding your cycle.

So why am I "Mad as Hell"? I recently showed up at a planned ride. It was 72 degrees out, and was overcast. There had been some sprinkles in surrounding towns, but not in the town where the run started. The ride was a supposed to be a short one—maybe 20 miles. The weather forecast was for "scattered showers."

About 15 bikes showed up for the event, and about 15 other people showed up in cages. Somehow (or somewhy) the people leading the event decided to cancel because of the "scattered showers" forecast. Not, mind you, because it was raining (because it was not), but because there was a forecast of scattered showers. I personally have never heard of an event being canceled because it "might" rain—but I guess these are the people my friend told me about, the ones with the water-soluble Harleys.

The Chairman and I

March 2014

I have had a very special relationship with Harley-Davidson. It started out normally enough, but grew into something much more; it has had a profound impact on my life, both personally and professionally

As a child I loved the freedom, the shiny red paint, and the chrome of my bicycle; needless to say, I really loved motorcycles. And my earliest memories are always Harleys. In my late teens I bought my first used Harley, which was followed by others through the years. In my mid-30s, I bought my first brand-new vehicle, a 1986 Harley FXRS Sport.

My relationship with Harley-Davidson was the same as everyone's—I was an enthusiast, a fan, an owner . . . a proud owner. My Harley was one of the joys of my life; between riding and working on the bike, I enjoyed many peaceful hours.

Then one day I read that the group of individuals who had "saved" Harley-Davidson, by buying it from AMF and putting it back on track, was "taking the company public." Having never bought stock before, I didn't fully understand the details; but what I did understand was that people would be able to buy stock in the company.

I approached my neighbor, a stockbroker, and asked how to get a few shares. About a week later he got back to me, with an answer I didn't much care for—he informed me that no stock was available, apparently everything offered had been bought by, or committed to, large insurance companies and mutual funds who were major investors.

This didn't sound right to me; wasn't the idea of "taking the company public" to raise money for Harley-Davidson, and allow the public to buy the stock? Being naïve, I decided to call Vaughn

Bealls, the Chairman of Harley-Davidson. (He's the man in the photo with President Reagan right before this article.) His secretary told me she'd check to see if he was in. What were the odds I'd actually get through? Likely I'd be transferred to an assistant to handle my call. Much to my surprise, the next voice I heard was not the secretary, it was the Chairman of the Board of Harley-Davidson!

I explained the situation to him, telling him I was a lifelong Harley enthusiast and an owner of one of the new Evolution-powered bikes. I also told him I had never bought stock in my life, was hoping to buy a few shares of HD, and had learned it was impossible to get any. He said he understood; or as he put it, I just wanted to own "a piece of the rock."

Mr. Bealls told me he had a block of stock set aside for employees of the The Motor Company, and as far as he knew they were not all committed. He said if that were so, they would be able to sell me a few shares. He told me he would follow up, thanked me for my call and for my loyalty, and ended the call. I wasn't certain I would ever hear back from him.

The next day, Mr. Bealls' secretary contacted me. When I heard her voice, I was certain it was to tell me that Mr. Bealls had tried his best, but that no stock was available. But no! He had actually secured 100 shares for me! I was amazed! I was just a customer, and yet the Chairman had intervened for me and extended this incredible benefit that was reserved for his employees!

100 shares at $11 each. And surprisingly, the next week, the stockbroker called . . . with another hundred shares. Between both, $2200; at this point in my life that was a fortune but I couldn't walk away from the opportunity to own a piece of Harley-Davidson.

While that was all surprising, what happened over the next eight years was even more surprising. Harley-Davidson became one of the darlings of Wall Street. The stock split four times, meaning my 200 shares became 400, then 800, then 1,600, and finally 3,200. And the shares were no longer trading at $11, they were trading at $55.

You could reach a quick conclusion and say, "Wow, a $2200 investment that turned into 3,200 shares at $55 each! A homerun!" And that would be a story about a huge financial windfall, but it goes much deeper.

There were two much more significant impacts. The first, as many of you know and the rest of you will you read on is, years later my friend and I opened a Harley-Davidson dealership; would this have ever happened if I didn't have the comfort level and confidence from my experience with Mr. Bealls? Maybe, but maybe not. And the other, my un-educated, gut-feel investment in Harley-Davidson led me to a lifetime of further investing.

Vaughn Bealls' gesture to accommodate me, a complete stranger but loyal customer, had a profound impact on the course of my life, changing it in ways I could never have imagined. And I've got to tell you, these are the kinds of things that happen in the Harley-Davidson family.

Lifelong Dream of Being a Harley Dealer

March 2014

When I sold my interest in Liberty Harley-Davidson in 2001, I heard from many customers who said something very much like, "Stu, I can't believe it. How could you leave? You have the best job in the world. I would do anything to have a job like yours."

It was pretty clear that many people thought I had the dream job. Probably thought that it was my lifelong dream to be a Harley dealer, and couldn't understand why I would walk away.

Let me start by telling you I have always loved motorcycles. I have been a motorcyclist for nearly 50 years, and love riding. I not only love motorcycles and riding, I love the world of motorcycling—the events, the people, the camaraderie. But the business?

Not only was becoming a Harley dealer not my lifelong dream, it had never even entered my mind. Long before my career in banking, I had worked in a motorcycle dealership. It was very much like a car dealership, with sales, service, and parts—the difference was, of course, the products sold had two wheels, not four. And Frank the dealer, who was my neighbor, worked like a dog—crazy long hours, always filling in for whoever was out that day, always explaining foul-ups to the customers. Didn't really look like a fun job to me.

In 1996 the bank where I worked for the past 25 years was sold, again—for the third time. As an employee it was not up to me to decide whether or not I liked the new owners; my job was to understand the new goals and strategies, and implement them. But for the first time in 25 years I found myself working for an organization that had unrealistic goals and expectations, and placed little value on employees or customers. I decided, at age 47, it was time to go.

But where? The original company had moved us to Moscow, PA (outside Scranton), but the new company asked me to manage an operation in Boston, so I was flying to Massachusetts every Monday morning, and returning every Friday. I liked Moscow, but Northeast Pennsylvaia was economically depressed, so we really couldn't stay.

In the meanwhile I had had some interesting conversations with my friend who owned a motorcycle repair shop in New Jersey. Harley-Davidson motorcycle repair. He was a brilliant individual who made a nice niche repairing motorcycles under the noses of his local Harley-Davidson dealers, who provided substandard services at exorbitant prices. (Please don't think I'm being judgmental; these particular Harley dealers have all since gone out of business.)

But he wanted more, he wanted to be an authorized Harley-Davidson dealer. It was his dream. Problem was, he had attempted to purchase a dealership in the past, and for unknown reasons wasn't approved. And it was a bit of a mystery. My friend had served honorably in the military, earned a college degree, was a successful business owner for several decades, had been president of a few statewide organizations—certainly credentials one would think would be acceptable.

But there was an intangible—he was a biker. And he looked like a biker. And he sounded like a biker. Now, Harley-Davidson had made a commitment to selecting only true motorcycle enthusiasts to own their dealerships. And my friend was more than just an enthusiast, he was a motorcycle fanatic. That, plus his credentials, should have made him a top candidate. The truth, unwritten though it may be, was that Harley-Davidson just plain didn't want any bikers as dealers.

They'll never admit it, but it was true. What they really wanted were professionals, lawyers, doctors, dentists, who happened to be motorcyclists . . . and had adequate capital to invest. While they certainly didn't mind selling motorcycles and parts to bikers, that wasn't who they wanted representing them.

Shortly after leaving the bank, my friend and I decided we would ride to Daytona for Biketoberfest (covered in detail elsewhere in this book); I needed time to think through my future. We spent a week riding down, hanging out, riding back. By the end of the week we had decided we would jointly apply, as partners, for a Harley-Davidson franchise.

My 25 years of experience in banking and finance, his 25 years in the automotive and motorcycle industry, both being serious motorcycle enthusiasts—how could Harley-Davidson not like our application? We spent a few weeks putting together every detail of our personal and financial lives for the application—to say that Harley fully researches their applicants would be an understatement.

A couple months later I got a phone call from the dealer development department at Harley advising me that our application had been approved! We were now approved to be Harley dealers! Unbelievable! Then the other shoe dropped—they explained that we were one of 900 approved applicants.

900! 900?? How could there be 900 approved applicants? So I asked just how many get dealerships in each year. They explained that in an average year there were five new dealers; and this included new dealerships and/or people buying existing dealerships. Five. Which meant that for all 900 applicants to get dealerships would take 180 years. (Hey man, we don't have 180 years to wait! We need a dealership now!)

They explained that the process was whenever a new dealer was needed, be it a new territory for Harley-Davidson, or the transfer or sale of an existing dealership, they would interview the top six applicants for that region of the country. So they asked me exactly what part of the country we were looking for, and they were unwilling to take "anywhere" for an answer—my friend and I both wanted out of the Northeast, so we selected the Carolinas.

A week later I called the dealer development department, and asked them if there were any developments. They told me I really didn't have to call, that they would call me when an opportunity arose. I called the next week. And the next. And the next.

And by the second month a different voice answered. Apparently our contact had been transferred to a different division in Harley-Davidson. I explained who we were to the new coordinator, who promptly told me that I really didn't need to call—they would call me when an opportunity arose. I called the next week. And the next. And the next.

A couple months later, unbelievable, a new voice again. And once again I introduced myself. And once again I got the same story, don't call us we'll call you . . . then something odd happened. As he was getting ready to end the call, he must've been looking at our application, he said, "Hmm, you fellas are from New Jersey?"

He caught me by surprise, I almost didn't know what to say. "Yes, we are from New Jersey, but we're looking to open in the Carolinas." Then, he came back with one of our worst fears, "We have an interesting opportunity in New Jersey."

We really wanted to move out of the cold winter climate, but equally important was our suspicion of this particular opportunity. We, the biker community, had followed with great interest the controversy between B&D Harley-Davidson in Rahway, NJ and Harley-Davidson. Seems The Motor Company had become extremely unhappy with the way this old-time dealership was being run, so unhappy in fact that they terminated the franchise.

This was big news for two reasons. First, it was the first time in the nearly hundred year history of Harley-Davidson that they had ever terminated a dealer. And second, the dealership was owned by a sick, diabetic old man—a double amputee confined to a wheelchair. A real human interest story, sick old man vs. corporate America—the kind that had been picked up by all three network news channels in New York City!

The biker community followed the goings on through the reporting of "Iron Horse Magazine" (which was not affiliated with "Iron Biker News" in any way). Long detailed articles about the origin and history of B&D Harley, their owners Bill and Doris, and what a great place it was to do business. It was a real public-relations disaster for Harley-Davidson.

When I told them we really didn't want to be involved with the B&D situation, they implored us to interview. They said there would be five other candidates interviewing, but they would love to talk with someone from New Jersey who knew the customers and the motorcycle scene. We figured interviewing with them would prepare us for the later interview we hoped to get; and, with five other applicants there was no way we would be selected. Besides, we feared if we didn't accept they would never consider us for another dealership.

We pulled out all the stops to impress Harley-Davidson. We wanted them to know that even though we might not be the proper applicants for the B&D territory, we were the kind of experienced professionals they needed, hopefully in the Carolinas.

We prepared a business plan that was as professional and as detailed as anything produced by a Wall Street firm. It ran the gamut from our philosophy, to our strategy and tactics, financial projections, risk assessments, demographics of the target area, marketing analysis, and more. We sent it to them early so they knew exactly what to expect from us. (They later told us it was the best business plan Harley-Davidson had ever received, and it had been passed around the senior executives, even to the chairman of the board.)

We needed to look the part. My tendency was to go in a three-piece vested banker suit; my partner convinced me this was over the top, and that we should show up like professionals in very nice "business casual." His tendency was to show up with his biker hair and beard; I convinced him this was over the top and we both went to barbers for professional haircuts and beard trims.

We showed up at 9AM for our one-hour interview in Newark. We were ushered in to a conference room and seated at the end of an enormous conference table, facing eight Harley-Davidson executives, none of whom we had ever met or spoken with before.

This was either a piss-your-pants, drop-your-bat, and run away moment—or it was a swing for the fences moment.

After brief introductions, the first question was "Why do you want to be Harley-Davidson dealers?" Not, how did we do our projections, how did we analyze the market, what experience do we have . . . just simply, why did we want to be Harley dealers.

We started telling the executives stories about our travels and our interactions with Harley-Davidson dealers through the years. We started telling them about the importance of dealerships being open seven days a week, providing service to stranded travelers, providing a welcoming haven for local riders.

We told them of our 1993 "Trip to Nowhere", an annual ride we would take on Fourth of July—the idea being to take a few days and go away from the beaches and other tourist destinations. In '93 our destination was Corning, New York—after all, who's going to Corning on Independence Day? It was about a 300 mile ride, through the beautiful forests of Pennsylvania and New York, and would put us close to Watkins Glen as well.

The ride went well, but as we pulled into the motel in Corning, I pulled in my clutch and the lever stayed in! It was about 4 PM on a Friday, so my partner, an excellent mechanic and pretty resourceful guy, began disassembling the side cover of my transmission. Within a half hour he had discovered that the fingers on the pivoting linkage actuator had broken—so when I pulled in the clutch lever the linkage didn't actually disengage the clutch.

The part needed was not an uncommon part, nor was it expensive. This sounded like pretty good news; just had to get it from a Harley dealer. Ho ho—this is where the fun begins. It was Friday night, and Independence Day was Sunday, so the holiday was being celebrated on Monday. Shouldn't be a problem—wake up in the morning and go to the local Harley dealer for the part.

Would you believe that every Harley-Davidson dealer within 150 miles closed for the entire three day weekend? Not a single dealer open on Saturday morning, and not a dealer opening until Monday. And not even a single dealer with an emergency number to call. The point of our story being, the time when dealers should be most available is when people are riding. Period.

(Did we wait until Monday to get the part? No. We found a gas station with an arc welder—unfortunately it was about 5 miles from the motel, and we had no way to move the motorcycle from the motel. So we welded the part and ground the weld, jumped on my partner's bike took it back and attempted to fit it. We went through this process six or seven times before it fit. We rode home on Sunday, a six-hour ride—I only pulled the clutch in three times on that ride. Good thing—that little bugger fractured roughly 80% through, and had I pulled the clutch one more time would have broken, again.)

And we related other stories to the Harley executives, and they asked us how we would solve those problems if we were dealers. We had a great conversation, shooting the breeze with people who were really interested.

As we exited in the room we were faced with a small crowd of pretty ticked-off looking applicants. It was 1 PM—what was scheduled as an hour interview turned into a four hour conversation of equals. I looked at my partner, and I don't remember who said it, but it was, "Holy shit, what just happened?" The next week Harley-Davidson notified us we were to be their newest New Jersey dealers.

I could spend pages talking about what it was like to open the dealership, but that is really the story of any new business. Trials, tribulations, opportunities, cost overruns, delays. But let me talk about just one thing, which further speaks to the fundamental nature of Harley-Davidson.

Like every owner of a new business, especially one building facilities, the money gets tight. No matter how well you plan, how well your contractors estimate, there are unforeseen costs. As we got to the 11th hour of the project, when the building was 99% complete, the staff had been selected and some were actually in the building putting away inventory and setting up the shop, we were trying hard not to look at our checking account—it was nearly drained, but we knew we would be opening soon and the Harley-Davidson name would attract enough customers to keep us afloat.

One afternoon, just a couple days before we opened the doors, someone came running into our office yelling "There's a Harley-Davidson tractor-trailer coming in!" We went out and found a large semi, all black and shiny, custom painted with orange Harley stripes and the bar and shield, and a smiling driver who said he had a delivery for us. We really weren't expecting anything.

He opened the back doors of the truck; he had 45 new Harleys in crates that were not part of our negotiated deal (we already had the few bikes that we were supposed to open with in our showroom), and the driver insisted they were for us. Right about then we were called to the phone, advised that our Harley District Manager was holding.

He told us the executives in Milwaukee knew we were opening in a few days, and "found" these 45 motorcycles for us, most of which were 95th Anniversary limited edition bikes! Suddenly, we had 45 of the most desirable bikes you can imagine to sell!

This was like Harley putting money directly into our checking account. And it speaks to commitment that Harley has to their dealers. This was the first, but not the last, time they surprised us this way. In the years since I sold my interest in Liberty Harley-Davidson, I have had the opportunity to work with over a dozen other motorcycle manufacturers; I have only encountered one other that treats their customers and dealers with that same kind of friendship and respect.

It may not have been my lifelong dream, but I will always be proud, and thankful, to have been a genuine Harley-Davidson dealer.

In late '98 when Tom McTamney and I opened Liberty Harley nearly all Harley dealers, certainly all in our area, were charging a large premium over MSRP for new Harleys. We had the novel idea that we would earn our customers' business the old fashioned way, fair prices and good service. We assumed they would love the idea of no "dealer markup", no up-front deposits, and no waiting lists. But it's tough to teach some old dogs new tricks.

—Stu, 2014

MSRP or Bust

Iron Biker News, January 1999

I'm sure it's no surprise to anyone that my partner, Tom McTamney (who also writes for this magazine), and I recently opened a Harley-Davidson dealership. It's certainly not a secret—we've been running one and two page ads for the last seven months.

As we unfortunately had to spend a year getting our facility ready, we had a very lot of time to contemplate exactly how we intended to do business. We talked about things like "best practices," "customer satisfaction" and "moments of truth." We made a conscious decision to differentiate our franchise along one dimension—customer satisfaction.

After all—in reality all motorcycle dealers have the same basic product to offer—motorcycles, motorcycle parts, service, aftermarket parts and clothing. There are a couple possibilities for a dealer to differentiate themselves—price (being the lowest), speed (being the fastest), effectiveness (doing the best work). We chose customer satisfaction—it's a little harder to define because the elements that may satisfy one customer may or may not satisfy another. So not only did we need to think about how to price and deliver products, and how to interact with the customer, we also needed to think about allowing for the differing expectations and needs of individual customers.

So we committed to developing a repair and service facility that would be unparalleled in our market, stocking a line of riding gear and accessories that meet our customers' needs, and developing a pricing policy that is fair and equitable. And herein lies my "Mad As Hell" for the month.

Motorcycle pricing, especially new Harley-Davidson pricing, is a very controversial topic—and is a serious sore point with many long time Harley riders. It seems that new riders (who are first-time Harley buyers) are usually very accepting of the current "market pricing" policies that are prevalent throughout the U.S. ("market pricing" means pricing at whatever the market will bear, even though that may be several thousand dollars over Manufacturers Suggested Retail Price). Many new buyers have told me the price of a Harley is whatever you have to pay, and besides the bikes keep their value, and furthermore they're glad to get a bike regardless of cost.

On the other hand, the overwhelming majority of long-time riders or repeat Harley buyers are seriously aggravated by dealers pricing over the MSRP. Many of these people have been riding Harleys for more than ten years, and were loyal to Harley and bought motorcycles even when the company was floundering and the quality of the bikes was substandard. They feel that their loyalty has not been repaid, and in fact they've been penalized by dealers who have tried to squeeze them for every cent—dealers who have blatantly ignored the fair price suggested by the Harley-Davidson Motor Company.

Given the opportunity to set our pricing wherever we wanted, Tom and I decided to "do the right thing." We decided to set our pricing at MSRP, and to take it one step further we decided we would have no waiting list. Instead of taking deposits, putting names on lists, and waiting for bikes to come in, we decided we would let the bikes come in, let the customers come in, and let the customers buy the bikes right off the showroom floor. What a novel idea!!

We figured both the new and seasoned riders would like this. Come in, find a bike you like, figure out how to pay for it, and ride it home. No 18 month wait—no $500 non-refundable deposit—no begging and groveling.

So how is it going? Well, most customers like it—and we are selling most of our bikes to people who leave smiling, on a new or nice used bike—a bike they got within a couple days of walking in. On the other hand, there are some customers who are really aggravated at us—who have stood in our showroom and yelled and screamed at us—who have told us that our policy is the stupidest most ridiculous thing they ever heard.

These are people who (I think) either aren't really committed to buying a bike, or who want to be sure they have a bike in the spring not the winter, or who don't have the money—or worst of all, have become so used to being treated badly that they've become accustomed to it. These people actually want us to take their money and make them wait.

What makes me angry is—they are actually pissed off at us for selling bikes off the floor at MSRP. They want to be overcharged and made to wait—if anybody can explain this to me, I sure would appreciate it (you can either write to me at Iron Biker, or at my e-mail address at the end of this article).

In the meanwhile if you like our "novel" idea of bike selling give me a call—if you're in my dealer territory I'll sell you a bike, and if you're not I'll do my best to hook you up with a dealer in your general vicinity who has a similar policy. On the other hand—if you're looking to put down a deposit, wait for 12 months to get a bike, and pay more than MSRP you too can give me a call—I won't sell you a bike, but I'll hook you up with a dealer who'll take your deposit, make you wait and charge you enough to make you regret it.

The Best Day of My Life

March 2014

I don't want you to think that being a Harley dealer was all headaches, it wasn't. Sure, there are all the challenges that every businessman faces, and sometimes those challenges make you wonder why you ever went in business, but there's also the other side.

When we first opened Liberty Harley-Davidson one of the things we wanted to ensure was that the customers would always have access to us, the dealers, as well as all of the staff members. We all wore name tags and/or had our first names embroidered on our shirts to put customers at ease.

We also positioned our offices, my partner's and mine, adjacent to the showroom floor, with plate glass windows so that customers could find us whenever they wanted. We had visited many Harley dealerships over the years; the hardest thing to find in any of them was always the dealer. Some dealers were absentee, others who were not had their office deep in the bowels of their buildings, where customers could never find them. We wanted none of it—if customers had a problem, we wanted to be the first to know, not the last.

One afternoon about two months after we opened, a giant of a man stuck his head in my door, "Are you the owner?" he growled in a gravelly voice.

His appearance took me aback and made me think of another man I met years before, when I was director of security and fraud prevention for the bank. One of my responsibilities was "straightening out" problems with customers; typically, this was customers who were difficult, or unmanageable, in some way or other.

In the late '70s and early '80s we were experiencing a construction boom in Atlantic City, with enormous casino hotels being erected. This drew contractors from around the country. And apparently one of the drywall contractors, who banked with us, had some unusual problem that the staff could not resolve. They asked for my help with Mr. Don Chuy.

I got him on the phone, and insisted he come in to meet so we could straighten out the problem. He was polite and soft-spoken. I remember thinking, as a result of his voice and his name, that he was most likely a Korean businessman.

The next day I walked into our conference room expecting to meet a typical Asian businessman. I think my jaw dropped when this mountain of a man slowly rose from his chair and extended his hand; I swear it was the size of a ham. No one had mentioned to me, or perhaps they didn't know, that Mr. Chuy, Don Chuy (who was not, incidentally, Asian, despite the name), played offensive guard for the Los Angeles Rams for seven seasons before becoming a contractor.

Anyway back to the giant in my door. Don Chuy was big, this man was bigger . . . and a lot meaner looking. Gravelly voice, wild eyes, unkempt hair and beard, looked like he could stare down a grizzly. "Are you the owner?"

My inner self wanted to jump out the window behind my desk . . . but I learned a long time ago—never show fear. I'm 6'1", and he towered over me. "Yes, I am. And you are . . ?" I said as I rose from my chair, coming around the edge of my desk and extending my hand to him.

He grabbed my hand, threw his other arm around me and started smothering me in a bear hug—then he started blubbering, "This is the best day of my life. Thank you so much. I've waited my whole life for this. I always dreamed I would get a new Harley some day." There were, and I shit you not, tears running down his cheeks.

Every couple months some customer would track down either my partner of I, and tell us it was the best day of their life. In the 25 years I spent in banking, many of them doing good things for customers, it was rare to even get a thank you. In the decade owning motorcycle stores selling brands other than Harley we've had a lot of satisfied, happy, even enthusiastic customers, but not like that. Harley riders are unique, they have a dedication and a passion for the brand which I don't believe is matched by any other brand on the planet. (Know anyone with a brand except Harley-Davidson tattooed on their body?)

The single best part of being a Harley dealer was not the rides, the trips to the Harley dealer show, the inside information, or any of the other cool benefits—the best part was these customers. Owning a dealership is a very lot of work and responsibility, more headaches than most people can imagine—long hours, employee issues, financial risk, sleepless nights . . . even though it happened only a few times a year, the customers who were having the best day of their life made it all worthwhile.

And them telling me always made it one of the best days of my life too.

We did several reviews of biker movies in the '80s and '90s. Most were done by me, but a couple by Gary, a couple by Stan, and a few from Iron Horse. Re-reading them now, I still think they are right on. This is a pretty darned good guide to biker movies from the '50s through the '90s. —Stu, 2014

Biker Movies

Iron Biker News

★★★★   Must see!
★★★   Also highly recommended.
★★   Fairly entertaining.
★   Have a few brews before ya watch these.
💣   Real bomb.

★ Angels Die Hard (1970)—William Smith, Dan Haggerty, Tom Baker. 60s vintage biker flick. Kind of weird plot and situations, but it is worth seeing. *Iron Horse*

★★ Beyond the Law (1992)—Supposedly true story of an Arizona cop who infiltrates the Arizona and California clubs, and whose investigation results in 200 arrests for drug trafficking and murder. Good performance by star Charlie Sheen, who plays a cop lured to the dark side. Once again however, a stereotypical treatment of bikers (as vicious morons). Some interesting inconsistencies (for those who would notice), like the rigid frame shovel the cop builds, which somehow incredibly metamorphosizes into a softail blockhead. *Stu*

★ The Born Losers (1967)—Tom Laughlin (as Billy Jack). The first Billy Jack film. Billy Jack is, as usual, avenging a rape. Yeah, the bikers are the baddies. Look for biker Bob Tessier playing Cue Ball. *Iron Horse*

💣* C.C. and Company (1970)—Joe Namath. Namath as a biker and Ann-Margret as his girlfriend, but you will find biker William Smith in this one too. I haven't seen this one in almost 20 years, and I ain't looking for it. *Stu*

★★★★ Easy Rider (1969)—This movie somehow defines the '60s, in an indescribable way (something like Woodstock or the Beatles). Two bikers chase the American dream—Peter Fonda is really hard to stomach (what an asshole), but Dennis Hopper comes across righteous, and Jack Nicholson (in a bit part) is as offbeat and entertaining as ever. Even though I couldn't stand Fonda, I have enjoyed this movie a half dozen times (and will admit after seeing it in '69 I raked and extended my wideglide 10 inches). *Great* soundtrack, great highway scenes, and a very different look at the '60s. *Stu*

★★ Electraglide in Blue (1973)—Robert Blake. No bikers in this one. Story about a sawed-off cycle cop with a giant ego. The cops ride hogs, and I enjoyed this flick. *Stu*

★ Harley Davidson and the Marlboro Man (1991)—I've watched this a couple times—it starts off good, then becomes a stupid and boring. Stars Mickey Rourke and Don Johnson. The redeeming quality is Rourke's acting (always strange—no exception here). The bike Rourke rides is righteous—it's an exact copy of his own scoot (but they made an 80c.i. copy for the flick cause his 98 inch stroker allegedly couldn't handle the low-speed camera shots). *Stu*

★ Hells Angels 69 (1969)—No plot to speak of, but if you're laid up on a snowy day with a sixpack you're sure to enjoy this one. *Iron Horse*

★★★ Hells Angels Forever (1983)—documentary. Iron Horse says this is an important flick; they can't recommend it enough and they say what ever you do, if you missed this one in the theaters get the tape. *Iron Horse*

★★ Hells Angels on Wheels (1967)—Jack Nicholson, Sonny Barger. A gas pump jockey fights and parties with the bikers. A pretty good flick. *Iron Horse*

💣* Hellriders (1985)—Adam West, Tina Loiuse (Yes indeed, TV's Batman and Gilligan's Ginger).

★ Knightriders (1983)—Ed Harris. Bad. Stupid. Embarassing. *Stu*

★★★ The Lazy Man's Zen—This was an hour special that ran on the Discovery Channel. If you can catch it, I think you'll like it. Interviews with real people, all focused on why they ride. These guys cover it all—Harleys (stock, chopped, touring), crotch rockets, Bonneville Salt Flats, etc. A very objective look at bikers and motorcyclists. *Stu*

★ Little Fauss and Big Halsey (1970)—Robert Redford, Michael J. Pollard. So-so story of two cycle racers, a self-centered braggart (Robert Redford) and his timid, gullible buddy (Michael J Pollard). *Stu*

💣* The Losers³ (1970)—good idea, rotten movie. A bunch of bikers go to Cambodia to fight from their armor-plated machinegun-totin' Yamaha 80s (cut me a break). There is a VW trike, complete with rocket launcher, but less you're gonna down a sixpack first I wouldn't waste my time on this one. *Stu*

★★★ The Loveless (1983)—Willem Dafoe. One of the best, probably the hardest to find. Willem Dafoe and Robert Gordon star in a 50s "bikers come to town" story. You won't be disappointed. *Iron Horse*

★★★ Mask (1985)—Cher, Sam Elliot. True story of a scooter trash mom trying to raise her deformed, terminally ill teenager. The only big-budget, major motion picture I know of that gives our lifestyle a fair shake. Charlotte was fantastic (should have gotten an Oscar), great performance by Sam Elliot, and the film actually did cop some Oscar nominations. See this one! *Stu*

---

³ As of 2014, this film has been re-named "Nam's Angels."

★★ On Any Sunday (1971)—documentary with Steve McQueen and Malcolm Smith. Covers every aspect of cycle racing, circa 1970—motocross, flat track, desert racing, road racing, a little ice racing, sidecars, drags and hill climbs. Worth seeing. *Stu*

★ On Any Sunday II (1981). Typical sequel, not as good as the original. Unless you are a real race fan, don't bother with this one. *Stu*

★★★ Roadside Prophets (1992)—John Doe, with bit parts by Timothy Leary, Arlo Guthrie, David Carradine and John Cusack. Offbeat story about a biker who gets seriously diverted trying to do a good deed for a downed bro. Makes me think of that line from the Janis Joplin song—"Freedom's just another word for nothin' left to lose." The acting's inconsistent, ranging from some terrific performances to some real melodrama. A strange but compelling story, and probably the best bike flick I've seen in a decade. See this one, if you can find it. *Stu*

★★ Run Angel Run (1969)—William Smith stars as a biker running from his bros, who thinks he ripped them off. Good story, and good stunt riding on a Sportster. *Stan*

★ Stone Cold (1991)—Really bad flick about a cop (Brian Bosworth), all decked out in his bleached blond moussed hair, designer jeans, and face shaved cleaner that a baby's behind, who incredibly infiltrates an outlaw club. This guy couldn't infiltrate kindergarten. Again, depiction of bikers as vicious imbeciles. A movie which really makes you question Hollywood's intelligence. *Stu*

◐ Streets of Fire (1984)—Michael Pare. The bikers play the bad guys in this "Rock 'N Roll Fable," where they kidnap a girl and her boyfriend sets out to rescue her. Iron Horse said this one was okay, so I rented it. There can't be more than four minutes of bike scenes (almost all filmed in low light) in the entire movie, and I was really disappointed. *Stu*

◐ Timerider (1983)—Great idea, lousy flick. Motocross rider and his bike are suddenly sent back 100 years to the old west. This is one of the most boring, disappointing films I have ever seen. Don't waste your time on it. Stu

★★ The Wild Angels (1966)—stars Peter Fonda (three years before Easy Rider), Bruce Dern, Nancy Sinatra, Venice Hells Angels. Real corny plot and real soap opera acting (if you thought Fonda was bad in Easy Rider, wait till you see this). But, Bruce Dern's performance is terrific and you get to see a bunch of genuine mid-60s West Coast hogs. *Stu*

★★★★ The Wild One (1954)—This is the original, the classic, and some say *the* biker movie. '50s "bikers take over the town" movie (inspired by actual events in Hollister, CA). We've all lived with both the "rebel without a cause" (Marlon Brando) and the "born loser" (Lee Marvin) images for the past 40 years—this film actually created the biker stereotype that we've all been branded with. This flick is just really dated, but you'd still probably enjoy it. *Stu*

The Coolest Dude

On Wheels

The Coolest Dude on Wheels

Stu Segal's Facebook Poll, March 2009

After I posted several pictures of my cars and bikes and I on Facebook, my friend Dennis Z. made a very nice comment that he thinks I am "the coolest dude on wheels." Not true, but got me thinking—who is the coolest dude on wheels?

I posted a poll on Facebook to see who people really think is the coolest. And the winners are:

Tied for *The Coolest Dude on Wheels*:

Steve McQueen, actor, rider. One cool dude.

Malcolm Forbes, the man who had it all . . . but what he loved most was riding his bikes.

Three-way tie for *Second Coolest*

Rollie Free

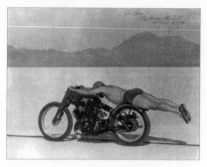

Rollie Free at 150mph! In 1948 he stripped to swim trunks, leather helmet and shoes, removed the seat from his Vincent Black Lightning, and lay on the rear fender to break the motorcycle land speed record. Perhaps the most famous motorcycle photo ever.

Paul Newman

After playing a racecar driver on film, Newman was hooked, going on to race cars the rest of his life. He holds the distinction of being the oldest driver to win a class at the 24 Hours of Daytona, aged 70 years and 8 days.

Burt Munro

68 year old New Zealander Burt Munro rode his 47 year old Indian 190mph in 1967, setting a world land speed record at Bonneville for under 1,000cc motorcycles. (Incidentally, the fastest any Indian motorcycle has ever gone, thus the movie title.)

Also in the running, but apparently lacking sufficient cool:

Marlon Brando

Peter Fonda

Jesse James

Danica Patrick

Pancho Villa

Elvis

Hunter S. Thompson

Jackie Stewart

T.E. Lawrence

Vin Diesel

Hunter S. Thompson

There has been a very lot written about motorcycles in the last sixty years, primarily in magazines, but occasionally in book form. Probably the best known book related to motorcycles is Hunter S. Thompson's "Hell's Angels." Written from Thompson's firsthand knowledge gained hanging with the club, it gave America a frightening look inside the world of a closed brotherhood, and rocketed the Hell's Angels to national infamy. Thompson's relationship with the Angels ended badly, with him being savagely stomped over a remark he made to one of the members.

Though he didn't write any more about bikes or bikers, he did continue to ride. And of course, he continued to write, taking the world by storm with his Gonzo Journalism.

In the mid '90s a motorcycle magazine commissioned an article from Thompson. It was supposed to be a road test, but what Thompson created endures as the finest piece of motorcycle journalism of the era. No one else understood the heart of a biker like Thompson, and no one else could express it in his unique style.

—Stu, 2014

Song of the Sausage Creature

Hunter S. Thompson, 1995

There are some things nobody needs in this world, and a bright red, hunchback, warp-speed 900cc café racer is one of them—but I want one anyway, and on some days I actually believe I need one. That is why they are dangerous.

Everybody has fast motorcycles these days. Some people go 150 miles an hour on two-lane blacktop roads, but not often. There are too many oncoming trucks and too many radar cops and too many stupid animals in the way. You have to be a little crazy to ride these super-torque high-speed crotch rockets anywhere except a racetrack—and even there, they will scare the whimpering shit out of you. There is, after all, not a pig's eye worth of difference between going head-on into a Peterbilt or sideways into the bleachers.

On some days you get what you want, and on others, you get what you need.

When Cycle World called me to ask if I would road-test the new Harley Road King, I got uppity and said I'd rather have a Ducati superbike. It seemed like a chic decision at the time, and my friends on the superbike circuit got very excited. "Hot damn," they said, "We will take it to the track and blow the bastards away."

Balls," I said. "Never mind the track. The track is for punks. We are Road People. We are Café Racers."

The Café Racer is a different breed, and we have our own situations. Pure speed in sixth gear on a 5,000-foot straightaway is one thing, but pure speed in third gear on a gravel-strewn downhill S-turn is quite another.

But we like it. A thoroughbred Café Racer will ride all night through a fog storm in freeway traffic to put himself into what somebody told him was the ugliest and tightest decreasing-radius turn since Genghis Khan invented the corkscrew.

Café Racing is mainly a matter of taste. It is an atavistic mentality, a peculiar mix of low style, high speed, pure dumbness, and overweening commitment to the Café Life and all its dangerous pleasures.... I am a Café Racer myself, on some days— and many nights for that matter—and it is one of my finest addictions....

I am not without scars on my brain and my body, but I can live with them. I still feel a shudder in my spine every time I see a Vincent Black Shadow, or when I walk into a public restroom and hear crippled men whispering about the terrifying Kawasaki Triple.... I have visions of compound femur fractures and large black men in white hospital suits holding me down on a gurney while a nurse called "Bess" sews the flaps of my scalp together with a stitching drill.

Ho, ho. Thank God for these flashbacks. The brain is such a wonderful instrument (until God sinks his teeth into it). Some people hear Tiny Tim singing when they go under, and others hear the song of the Sausage Creature.

When the Ducati turned up in my driveway, nobody knew what to do with it. I was in New York, covering a polo tournament, and people had threatened my life. My lawyer said I should give myself up and enroll in the Federal Witness Protection Program. Other people said it had something to do with the polo crowd.

The motorcycle business was the last straw. It had to be the work of my enemies, or people who wanted to hurt me. It was the vilest kind of bait, and they knew I would go for it.

Of course. You want to cripple the bastard? Send him a 130-mph café racer. And include some license plates, so he'll think it's a streetbike. He's queer for anything fast.

Which is true. I have been a connoisseur of fast motorcycles all my life. I bought a brand-new 650 BSA Lightning when it was billed as "the fastest motorcycle ever tested by Hot Rod magazine." I have ridden a 500-pound Vincent through traffic on the Ventura Freeway with burning oil on my legs and run the Kawa 750 triple through Beverly Hills at night with a head full of acid.... I have ridden with Sonny Barger and smoked weed in biker bars with Jack Nicholson, Grace Slick, Ron Zigler, and my infamous old friend, Ken Kesey, a legendary Café Racer.

Some people will tell you that slow is good—and it may be, on some days—but I am here to tell you that fast is better. I've always believed this, in spite of the trouble it's caused me. Being shot out of a cannon will always be better than being squeezed out of a tube. That is why God made fast motorcycles, Bubba....

So when I got back from New York and found a fiery red rocket-style bike in my garage, I realized I was back in the road-testing business.

The brand-new Ducati 900 Campione del Mundo Desmodue Supersport double-barreled magnum Café Racer filled me with feelings of lust every time I looked at it. Others felt the same way. My garage quickly became a magnet for drooling superbike groupies. They quarreled and bitched at each other about who would be first to help me evaluate my new toy.... And I did, of course, need a certain spectrum of opinions, besides my own, to properly judge this motorcycle. The Woody Creek Perverse Environmental Testing Facility is a long way from Daytona or even top-fuel challenge sprints on the Pacific Coast Highway, where teams of big-bore Kawasakis and Yamahas are said to race head-on against each other in death-defying games of chicken at 100 miles an hour....

No. Not everybody who buys a high-dollar torque-brute yearns to go out in a ball of fire on a public street in L.A. Some of us are decent people who want to stay out of the emergency room, but still blast through neo-gridlock traffic in residential districts whenever we feel like it.... For that we need fine machinery.

Which we had—no doubt about that. The Ducati people in New Jersey had opted, for reasons of their own, to send me the 900SP for testing—rather than their 916 crazy-fast, state-of-the-art superbike track racer. It was far too fast, they said—and prohibitively expensive—to farm out for testing to a gang of half-mad Colorado cowboys who think they're world-class Café Racers.

The Ducati 900 is a finely engineered machine. My neighbors called it beautiful and admired its racing lines. The nasty little bugger looked like it was going 90 miles an hour when it was standing still in my garage.

Taking it on the road, though, was a genuinely terrifying experience. I had no sense of speed until I was going 90 and coming up fast on a bunch of pickup trucks going into a wet curve along the river. I went for both brakes, but only the front one worked, and I almost went end over end. I was out of control staring at the tailpipe of a U.S. Mail truck, still stabbing frantically at my rear brake pedal, which I just couldn't find.... I am too tall for these New Age roadracers; they are not built for any rider taller than five-nine, and the rearset brake pedal was not where I thought it would be. Midsize Italian pimps who like to race from one café to another on the boulevards of Rome in a flat-line prone position might like this, but I do not.

I was hunched over the tank like a person diving into a pool that got emptied yesterday. Whacko! Bashed into the concrete bottom, flesh ripped off, a Sausage Creature with no teeth, f-cked-up for the rest of its life.

We all love Torque, and some of us have taken it straight over the high side from time to time -- and there is always Pain in that.... But there is also Fun, in the deadly element, and Fun is what you get when you screw this monster on. BOOM! Instant takeoff, no screeching or squawking around like a fool with your teeth clamping down on your tongue and your mind completely empty of everything but fear.

No. This bugger digs right in and shoots you straight down the pipe, for good or ill.

On my first takeoff, I hit second gear and went through the speed limit on a two-lane blacktop highway full of ranch traffic. By the time I went up to third, I was going 75 and the tach was barely above 4,000 rpm....

And that's when it got its second wind. From 4,000 to 6,000 in third will take you from 75 to 95 in two seconds -- and after that, Bubba, you still have fourth, fifth, and sixth. Ho, ho.

I never got into sixth, and I didn't get deep into fifth. This is a shameful admission for a full-bore Café Racer, but let me tell you something, old sport: This motorcycle is simply too goddamn fast to ride at speed in any kind of normal road traffic unless you're ready to go straight down the centerline with your nuts on fire and a silent scream in your throat.

When aimed in the right direction at high speed, though, it has unnatural capabilities. This I unwittingly discovered as I made my approach to a sharp turn across some railroad tracks, saw that I was going way too fast and that my only chance was to veer right and screw it on totally, in a desperate attempt to leapfrog the curve by going airborne.

It was a bold and reckless move, but it was necessary. And it worked: I felt like Evil Knievel as I soared across the tracks with the rain in my eyes and my jaws clamped together in fear. I tried to spit down on the tracks as I passed them, but my mouth was too dry.... I landed hard on the edge of the road and lost my grip for a moment as the Ducati began fishtailing crazily into oncoming traffic. For two or three seconds I came face to face with the Sausage Creature....

But somehow the brute straightened out. I passed a school bus on the right and then got the bike under control long enough to gear down and pull off into an abandoned gravel driveway where I stopped and turned off the engine. My hands had seized up like claws and the rest of my body was numb. I felt nauseous and I cried for my mama, but nobody heard, then I went into a trance for 30 or 40 seconds until I was finally able to light a cigarette and calm down enough to ride home. I was too hysterical to shift gears, so I went the whole way in first at 40 miles an hour.

Whoops! What am I saying? Tall stories, ho, ho.... We are motorcycle people; we walk tall and we laugh at whatever's funny. We shit on the chests of the Weird....

But when we ride very fast motorcycles, we ride with immaculate sanity. We might abuse a substance here and there, but only when it's right. The final measure of any rider's skill is the inverse ratio of his preferred Traveling Speed to the number of bad scars on his body. It is that simple: If you ride fast and crash, you are a bad rider. If you go slow and crash, you are a bad rider. And if you are a bad rider, you should not ride motorcycles.

The emergence of the superbike has heightened this equation drastically. Motorcycle technology has made such a great leap forward. Take the Ducati. You want optimum cruising speed on this bugger? Try 90 mph in fifth at 5,500 rpm—and just then, you see a bull moose in the middle of the road. WHACKO. Meet the Sausage Creature.

Or maybe not: The Ducati 900 is so finely engineered and balanced and torqued that you can do 90 mph in fifth through a 35-mph zone and get away with it. The bike is not just fast—it is extremely quick and responsive, and it will do amazing things.... It is a little like riding the original Vincent Black Shadow, which would outrun an F-86 jet fighter on the takeoff runway, but at the end, the F-86 would go airborne and the Vincent would not, and there was no point in trying to turn it. WHAMO! The Sausage Creature strikes again.

There is a fundamental difference, however, between the old Vincents and the new breed of superbikes. If you rode the Black Shadow at top speed for any length of time, you would almost certainly die. That is why there are not many life members of the Vincent Black Shadow Society. The Vincent was like a bullet that went straight; the Ducati is like the magic bullet that went sideways and hit JFK and the Governor of Texas at the same time. It was impossible. But so was my terrifying sideways leap across railroad tracks on the 900SP. The bike did it easily with the grace of a fleeing tomcat. The landing was so easy I remember thinking, goddamnit, if I had screwed it on a little more I could have gone a lot further.

Maybe this is the new Café Racer macho. My bike is so much faster than yours that I dare you to ride it, you lame little turd. Do you have the balls to ride this BOTTOMLESS PIT OF TORQUE?

That is the attitude of the New Age superbike freak, and I am one of them. On some days they are about the most fun you can have with your clothes on. The Vincent just killed you a lot faster than a superbike will. A fool couldn't ride the Vincent Black Shadow more than once, but a fool can ride a Ducati 900 many times, and it will always be bloodcurdling kind of fun. That is the Curse of Speed which has plagued me all my life. I am a slave to it. On my tombstone they will carve, "IT NEVER GOT FAST ENOUGH FOR ME."

T.E. Lawrence

Perhaps one of the fines pieces of motor journalism ever, "The Road" was written by T.E. Lawrence, better known as "Lawrence of Arabia." Nearly everyone knows Lawrence rode, as the epic film of his time in Arabia opens with the unforgettable scene of his deadly motorcycle crash. What few people know is that Lawrence loved motorcycling, finding the solace he was unable to find elsewhere in the power and speed of his beloved Brough Superiors.

Lawrence owned seven Brough Superiors, which were known as "The Rolls Royce of Motorcycles," in his lifetime. Each one was custom built by George Brough to fit Lawrence' 5'5" stature. (He referred to them as Boanerges, his "Sons of Thunder," the name Jesus used to refer to James and John.)

At the time Lawrence penned "The Road" he had returned from Arabia, had left the Army, and sought a life of anonymity. He enlisted in the RAF under an assumed name ("T.E. Ross," but apparently they all knew who he was, and respected his privacy). He was living the quiet life of an aviation engineer, rejecting the fame the world thrust upon him, and finding joy in the freedom and speed and solitude of his motorcycle rides.

—Stu, 2014

The Road

From *The Mint,* by T.E. Lawrence, 1928

The extravagance in which my surplus emotion expressed itself lay on the road. So long as roads were tarred blue and straight; not hedged; and empty and dry, so long I was rich.

Nightly I'd run up from the hangar, upon the last stroke of work, spurring my tired feet to be nimble. The very movement refreshed them, after the day-long restraint of service. In five minutes my bed would be down, ready for the night: in four more I was in breeches and puttees, pulling on my gauntlets as I walked over to my bike, which lived in a garage-hut, opposite. Its tyres never wanted air, its engine had a habit of starting at second kick: a good habit, for only by frantic plunges upon the starting pedal could my puny weight force the engine over the seven atmospheres of its compression.

Boanerges' first glad roar at being alive again nightly jarred the huts of Cadet College into life. 'There he goes, the noisy bugger,' someone would say enviously in every flight. It is part of an airman's profession to be knowing with engines: and a thoroughbred engine is our undying satisfaction. The camp wore the virtue of my Brough like a flower in its cap. Tonight Tug and Dusty came to the step of our hut to see me off. 'Running down to Smoke, perhaps?' jeered Dusty; hitting at my regular game of London and back for tea on fine Wednesday afternoons.

Boa is a top-gear machine, as sweet in that as most single-cylinders in middle. I chug lordlily past the guard-room and through the speed limit at no more than sixteen. Round the bend, past the farm, and the way straightens. Now for it. The engine's final development is fifty-two horse-power. A miracle that all this docile strength waits behind one tiny lever for the pleasure of my hand.

Another bend: and I have the honour of one of England' straightest and fastest roads. The burble of my exhaust unwound like a long cord behind me. Soon my speed snapped it, and I heard only the cry of the wind which my battering head split and fended aside. The cry rose with my speed to a shriek: while the air's coldness streamed like two jets of iced water into my dissolving eyes. I screwed them to slits, and focused my sight two hundred yards ahead of me on the empty mosaic of the tar's gravelled undulations.

Like arrows the tiny flies pricked my cheeks: and sometimes a heavier body, some house-fly or beetle, would crash into face or lips like a spent bullet. A glance at the speedometer: seventy-eight. Boanerges is warming up. I pull the throttle right open, on the top of the slope, and we swoop flying across the dip, and up-down up-down the switchback beyond: the weighty machine launching itself like a projectile with a whirr of wheels into the air at the take-off of each rise, to land lurchingly with such a snatch of the driving chain as jerks my spine like a rictus.

Once we so fled across the evening light, with the yellow sun on my left, when a huge shadow roared just overhead. A Bristol Fighter, from Whitewash Villas, our neighbour aerodrome, was banking sharply round. I checked speed an instant to wave: and the slip-stream of my impetus snapped my arm and elbow astern, like a raised flail. The pilot pointed down the road towards Lincoln. I sat hard in the saddle, folded back my ears and went away after him, like a dog after a hare. Quickly we drew abreast, as the impulse of his dive to my level exhausted itself.

The next mile of road was rough. I braced my feet into the rests, thrust with my arms, and clenched my knees on the tank till its rubber grips goggled under my thighs. Over the first pot-hole Boanerges screamed in surprise, its mud-guard bottoming with a yawp upon the tyre. Through the plunges of the next ten seconds I clung on, wedging my gloved hand in the throttle lever so that no bump should close it and spoil our speed. Then the bicycle wrenched sideways into three long ruts: it swayed dizzily, wagging its tail for thirty awful yards. Out came the clutch, the engine raced freely: Boa checked and straightened his head with a shake, as a Brough should.

The bad ground was passed and on the new road our flight became birdlike. My head was blown out with air so that my ears had failed and we seemed to whirl soundlessly between the sun-gilt stubble fields. I dared, on a rise, to slow imperceptibly and glance sideways into the sky. There the Bif was, two hundred yards and more back. Play with the fellow? Why not? I slowed to ninety: signalled with my hand for him to overtake. Slowed ten more: sat up. Over he rattled. His passenger, a helmeted and goggled grin, hung out of the cock-pit to pass me the 'Up yer' Raf randy greeting.

They were hoping I was a flash in the pan, giving them best. Open went my throttle again. Boa crept level, fifty feet below: held them: sailed ahead into the clean and lonely country. An approaching car pulled nearly into its ditch at the sight of our race. The Bif was zooming among the trees and telegraph poles, with my scurrying spot only eighty yards ahead. I gained though, gained steadily: was perhaps five miles an hour the faster. Down went my left hand to give the engine two extra dollops of oil, for fear that something was running hot: but an overhead Jap twin, super-tuned like this one, would carry on to the moon and back, unfaltering.

We drew near the settlement. A long mile before the first houses I closed down and coasted to the cross-roads by the hospital. Bif caught up, banked, climbed and turned for home, waving to me as long as he was in sight. Fourteen miles from camp, we are, here: and fifteen minutes since I left Tug and Dusty at the hut door.

I let in the clutch again, and eased Boanerges down the hill along the tram-lines through the dirty streets and up-hill to the aloof cathedral, where it stood in frigid perfection above the cowering close. No message of mercy in Lincoln. Our God is a jealous God: and man's very best offering will fall disdainfully short of worthiness, in the sight of Saint Hugh and his angels.

Remigius, earthy old Remigius, looks with more charity on and Boanerges. I stabled the steel magnificence of strength and speed at his west door and went in: to find the organist practising something slow and rhythmical, like a multiplication table in notes on the organ. The fretted, unsatisfying and unsatisfied lace-work of choir screen and spandrels drank in the main sound. Its surplus spilled thoughtfully into my ears.

By then my belly had forgotten its lunch, my eyes smarted and streamed. Out again, to sluice my head under the White Hart's yard-pump. A cup of real chocolate and a muffin at the teashop: and Boa and I took the Newark road for the last hour of daylight. He ambles at forty-five and when roaring his utmost, surpasses the hundred. A skittish motor-bike with a touch of blood in it is better than all the riding animals on earth, because of its logical extension of our faculties, and the hint, the provocation, to excess conferred by its honeyed untiring smoothness. Because Boa loves me, he gives me five more miles of speed than a stranger would get from him.

At Nottingham I added sausages from my wholesaler to the bacon which I'd bought at Lincoln: bacon so nicely sliced that each rasher meant a penny. The solid pannier-bags behind the saddle took all this and at my next stop a (farm) took also a felt-hammocked box of fifteen eggs. Home by Sleaford, our squalid, purse-proud, local village. Its butcher had six penn'orth of dripping ready for me. For months have I been making my evening round a marketing, twice a week, riding a hundred miles for the joy of it and picking up the best food cheapest, over half the country side.

afterword

The Golden Age of Motorcycling

Stu Segal, February 2014

In my early years of motorcycling, the '60s, I spent more time fixing my bike than riding it. And I don't mean "customizing," I mean repairing. I could remove a Harley engine and trans in my sleep. Torque wrench? When you've done head bolts for the hundredth time, your forearm is your torque wrench. And it wasn't just me, it was everyone; if you weren't either mechanical enough or clever enough to figure out how to keep a bike running, this just wasn't the thing for you.

We were adventurous youths, we wanted to go places. We had no Harley dealer in Atlantic City or nearby, so we would make excursions to the "big" dealers, the places that stocked accessories and chrome. A couple times a year we would ride to Rising Sun Harley-Davidson (it was really H-D of Philadelphia, on Rising Sun Avenue), and once a year to the "Chrome King," B&D Harley-Davidson in Rahway, NJ.

Today we wouldn't give a sixty mile ride to Philadelphia or a hundred mile ride up the Parkway to North Jersey a second thought. But back then, what a difference! We always set out with our bikes running fine, and tried to do it in decent weather. And it always took days.

Yes, *days*, to make what should have been a four-hour round trip. Welcome to the world of "Zen and Art of Motorcycle Maintenance." Flat tires, broken clutch cables, carburetor fires— you name it, we had it. These one-day trips always turned into two or three days, for several reasons. First, the bikes—completely undependable by today's standards. Second, the motorcycle dealers—think any of them every heard of convenient hours or customer satisfaction in the '60s? Third, being on your own—no cell phones, no roadside assistance for motorcycles.

Then of course, when the bikes *were* running you had to be able to ride them, no easy task in a world that was both anti-chopper and anti-rebellious youth. Yes, law enforcement really did lay in wait for us; yes, they really did radio ahead to the next town. Which left us either skulking around the streets individually, darting from alley to alley, constantly making right-hand turns to stay off the main drag and try to fly under the radar, or riding in groups because we felt there was strength in numbers (always backfired—just attracted more heat).

Over time we changed and, the world changed. The planet grew smaller and demands on our time grew larger. Fifty channels of TV to let us see the rest of the world, beepers so the world could find us. Ultimately the ubiquity of both the internet and cell phones, shrinking the world to a size we all could grasp, and giving us access to the entire universe of human knowledge, anytime, anywhere. And as the world changed so did design, manufacturing, customer expectations, and consumer products. No longer were we satisfied with shopping six days a week plus Thursday night, or banking Monday through Friday. We needed everything available, all the time.

No longer were we satisfied with changing our own flat tires, we deserved roadside assistant. As a matter of fact, no longer were we willing to accept vehicular breakdowns at all; engineers met the challenge and over decades began designing cars that, compared to the first seven decades of automobiles, were relatively trouble free. But it didn't stop there. Consumer demand for high quality pervaded nearly every manifestation of consumer products . . . including, yep, motorcycles.

Over the decades I owned some great motorcycles—Harleys, Triumphs, BSAs . . . I even once got to ride a Vincent, yes a legendary Vincent, 1,000ccs of fire-breathing fury. But all these bikes were, by our current standards, beasts—crude, slow (though we didn't think so at the time), dangerous, undependable.

Todays' motorcycles are simply amazing. In so many respects. First, there is the dependability; no more working on the bike two hours for every hour of riding. If maintained properly, and not abused, modern motorcycles rarely break down. And if they do, there's real live roadside assistance. And then there is, of course, the universal tool that fixes everything, the cellphone . . . so there is no more being stranded by the side of the road for hours.

And when I say " modern motorcycles rarely break down ," I'm not talking about one or two special brands, I'm talking about bikes in general from major manufacturers. Harley, Honda, Triumph, Victory, Ducati, BMW, Yamaha, etc. The quality they build today is what dreams were made of in the '60s.

Then there's the selection, also amazing. When I started riding there was one, one, American motorcycle company, and at the time they were building substandard products and teetering on the brink of extinction. Now, not only has Harley turned around the product and the company, building bikes admired and sought after round the world, we have other, viable American brands. Victory, built by Polaris Industries, has been making quality heavyweight American motorcycles for the past 15 years, and last year Polaris re-launched the storied Indian brand. Erik Buell Racing in Wisconsin is building genuine sport bikes, right here in America. *Four* brands of American motorcycles, something we haven't seen in three quarters of a century!

But it doesn't end with American motorcycles. The European and Asian brands are better, and stronger, than ever before. BMW from Germany, incorporating all the high tech from the company's automotive research, Ducati from Italy, now with the muscle of Volkswagen behind them, and Triumph, reborn in Coventry and better than anything the company built back in the day. The Japanese, still engineering and building outstanding bikes, though changes in the world economy and the relative value of the yen don't give them the price advantage they once enjoyed.

The range of bikes, be they domestic or foreign, is also amazing. Big touring bikes, sport touring, cruisers, traditional bikes (naked), sportbikes, adventure touring. Even factory choppers with raked and extended forks, engineered properly to handle perfectly, and completely street legal! Whether you want to travel the Pan-American Highway through Central and South America, ride the twisties of the Alps, of just cruise to your local café, there's a bike for you.

The performance of these bikes is beyond what anyone's imagination could have ever conjured up back in the '60s. 0-60 in under 3 seconds? I suppose you could buy a sixteen-cylinder, thousand horsepower Bugatti Veyron for a cool $2 million ... or ... pick up one of a dozen bikes from major manufacturers like Ducati, Honda, BMW and others for $10-20K. Want to go to the racetrack? Need a bike that will stick like glue just like the Superbike or MotoGP'ers? Not a problem, also available in the $10-15K range. And *all* these bikes are street legal, come with full warranty, and are as dependable as your daily driver.

The clothing and other gear available is also amazing. No more freezing, being soaked, sweating. No more engineer boots and jeans to "protect" you from a mishap. There is a huge selection of outerwear made from high tech materials that protect from the wind, the rain, as well as impact and abrasion. Summer gear with cooling properties. Boots, gloves, helmets with built-in sunglasses. Heated gear. And the list goes on.

The best part perhaps? The social environment in American has changed in the past 35 years—motorcycling is no longer stigmatized, it has become widespread, and acceptable. My own experience is that you are no more likely to be stopped by law enforcement when riding a bike that when driving a car. The exception being, of course, if you're riding or behaving like a wild man.

When I get on a bike now, it's like a dream come true. The bike starts; no more kicking until the sweat is running down my neck. It gets me where I'm going; no more broken chains and seized engines. If I want to push it through turns like Michael Schumacher or come off the line like E.J. Potter, no problem. And again, maybe best of all, no law enforcement waiting in the bushes to nab me every time my front wheel hits the highway.

Right now it all works . . . this really is as good as it gets. Better than it's ever been in the 50 years I've been riding—this really is the golden age of motorcycling in America.

Index of Articles, by Year

Index of Photographs

Cover —Circa 1968. Author on his first Harley, a '51 wishbone frame with a '58 panhead engine. Horn-rimmed glasses and Converse ALL★STARS.

Page 15 — Circa 1971. Author with a 36" extended springer fork on a rigid-frame panhead. Yes, we really did build these forks ourselves, using radius rods from old Ford straight front axles.

Page 65 — Circa 1970. E.J. Potter, "The Michigan Madman" (1941-2012), on his V-8 Chevy powered bike, "The Widowmaker." Potter toured dragstrips of the country in the '60s and '70s, showing us two things. Speed, power, noise and action are cool, and, nobody had bigger cojones than the mild looking bespectacled E.J. Potter, who rode the beast to 170mph+ in the quarter mile.

Page 91 — Early 1990s. "Let Freedom Roar." Rolling Thunder ride to the NYC memorial. Gathering at Liberty State Park in New Jersey, the World Trade Center in the background. Rashmika and I were at the ride. Photo by Pulsating Paula.

Page 105 — Unknown rider entering the tunnel on Iron Mountain Road, Mount Rushmore in the background.

Page 131 — George W. Bush greeting Rolling Thunder riders.

Page 141 — Wheelie!

Page 153 — Steve McQueen's incredible jump over a barbed wire fence in the 1963 film, "The Great Escape." Okay, so somehow the military BMW he stole morphed into a Triumph. And oh yeah, the jump was actually made by McQueen's friend, Bud Ekins.

Page 167 — May 16, 1987. President Ronald Reagan with H-D Chairman Vaughn Bealls, at Harley's million square foot plant in York, PA. This was subsequent to President Reagan releasing the tariffs on foreign motorcycles as requested by Harley. The Motor Company had roared back, improved their quality, expanded their line, and were able to compete, and beat, the competition on equal footing. Reagan was addressing the work force at the Harley-Davidson plant that day.

Page 189 — 1991. Mickey Rourke and Don Johnson from the film "Harley-Davidson and the Marlboro Man." It should be noted Rourke rode a replica of his own bike that was built for the film.

Page 197 — Circa 1964. Andy Griffith and Don Knotts as "Andy Taylor" and "Barney Fife."

Page 203 — 2014. A photograph of some of the biker literature on the coffee table in our living room. Including "Iron Biker News", Hunter S. Thompson's "Hells Angel's", Lenny Mandel's "From Cross to Cross", "AWOL" from England, "The Art of the Motorcycle" from the Guggenheim, et al. And that is a genuine 1940 OHV intake wrench lying on top.

Page 219 — 1953. Marlon Brando and Mary Murphy. "The Wild One," Columbia Pictures.

About the Author

Stu Segal is a voracious consumer of film and literature; he writes, rides motorcycles, juggles balls, clubs & knives, listens to rock 'n roll and plays drums. You can find him annually at the World Science Fiction Convention, the Westminster Kennel Club Show, rock concerts, motorcycle events, on the internet, and occasionally in the French Quarter.

Stu was raised in Atlantic City, New Jersey. He went into banking as a coin wrapping clerk, and concluded a banking career 24 years later as vice president of a global bank, and on the Board of Directors of the New York Cash Exchange. He subsequently opened motorcycle dealerships selling Harley-Davidsons, Triumphs, Hondas, Buells, Victorys and more.

Stu has been riding for nearly a half century—beginning on British bikes, he quickly graduated to Harley-Davidsons, which he rode exclusively for 35 years. Stu has owned many motorcycles over the years; he still rides and keeps his bikes serviced, fueled, and ready to go at all times.

Books by Stu Segal
Available at Amazon, Barnes & Noble, and all fine bookstores:

How to Read Drum Music
Too Young for a Heart Attack
Rants, Rumbles and Roars

You can reach Stu at stu.segal@ssegal.net

Made in the USA
Middletown, DE
10 November 2014